Editor
Stephanie Buehler, Psy.D.

Editorial Project Manager
Ina Massler Levin, M.A.

Editor-in-Chief
Sharon Coan, M.S. Ed.

Illustrator
Sue Fullam

Cover Artist
Jessica Orlando

Art Coordinator
Denice Adorno

Art Director
Richard D'Sa

Imaging
Alfred Lau
Ralph Olmedo, Jr.

Product Manager
Phil Garcia

Publishers
Rachelle Cracchiolo, M.S. Ed.
Mary Dupuy Smith, M.S. Ed.

Poetry Writing

Grades 6-8

Written by

Kimberly A. Williams

Teacher Created Materials, Inc.
6421 Industry Way
Westminster, CA 92683
www.teachercreated.com
ISBN-1-57690-998-0

©2000 Teacher Created Materials, Inc.
Reprinted, 2004
Made in U.S.A.

Table of Contents

Table of Contents (cont.)

How to Use This Book

Poetry Writing—Grades 6–8 is for teachers who want to teach students to love poetry. It is for teachers who love poetry themselves. It is for teachers who may not love poetry but want to develop an appreciation of the form, both for themselves and for their students. This book is for students—to help them explore the craft of poetry by reading, understanding, and writing poems that express who they are and who they want to be.

The first section of the book offers step-by-step skill-building lessons that teach students to become proficient in the techniques that poets use. Lessons are also included to help students generate ideas for their own poetry. Teachers can teach each skill-building lesson or pick and choose those which are most appropriate for the needs of their students.

Following the skill-building lessons, students learn to apply their skills by writing original poetry. Each type of poem that students will write is accompanied by a teacher's guide, a student assignment work sheet, sample poems, comprehension questions, and other supplementary materials. The sample poems include commentary so that the students can attend to the use of language. Many of the comprehension work sheets also include an idea bank to help students generate ideas for writing their own poems.

The final section of the book offers several suggestions for celebrating student work, including the creation of a poetry portfolio and accompanying highlight notes modeled after the running commentary included with the student samples.

Sharing poetry with students may open new avenues for both you as a teacher and your students as writers. When students can understand and relate to poetry as readers, they experience greater success as poets themselves. Develop a love of poetry in your students—your rewards will be endless!

Acknowledgements

The author would like to especially thank the following students for the use of their poetry as samples: Jenny Schatz, Jeff Connor, Chris Sanborn, Karen Gostomski, Michelle Barbieri, Megan Marshall, Erin Troy, Maggie Mackinnon, Colleen McGrath, Heidi Buchanan, Erin Seippel.

Standards for Writing
Grades 6–8

Accompanying the major activities of this book are references to the basic standards and benchmarks for writing that will be met by successful performance of the activities. Each specific standard and benchmark will be referred to by the appropriate letter and number from the following collection. For example, a basic standard and benchmark identified as **1A** would be as follows:

Standard 1: Demonstrates competence in the general skills and strategies of the writing process

Benchmark A: Prewriting: Uses a variety of prewriting strategies (e.g., makes outlines, uses published pieces as writing models, constructs critical standards, brainstorms, builds background knowledge)

A basic standard and benchmark identified as **4B** would be as follows:

Standard 4: Gathers and uses information for research purposes

Benchmark B: Uses the card catalog to locate books for research topics

Clearly, some activities will address more than one standard. Moreover, since there is a rich supply of activities included in this book, some will overlap in the skills they address, and some, of course, will not address every single benchmark within a given standard. Therefore, when you see these standards referenced in the activities, refer to this section for complete descriptions.

Although virtually every state has published its own standards and every subject area maintains its own lists, there is surprising commonality among these various sources. For the purposes of this book, we have elected to use the collection of standards synthesized by John S. Kendall and Robert J. Marzano in their book, *Content Knowledge: A Compendium of Standards and Benchmarks for K–12 Education* (Second Edition, 1997) as illustrative of what students at various grade levels should know and be able to do. The book is published jointly by McRel (Mid-continent Regional Educational Laboratory, Inc.) and ASCD (Association for Supervision and Curriculum Development). (Used by permission of McRel. 2550 S. Parker Road., Suite 500, Aurora, CO 89914; http://www.mcrel.org.)

Language Arts

1. Demonstrates competence in the general skills and strategies of the writing process

2. Demonstrates competence in the stylistic and rhetorical aspects of writing

3. Uses grammatical and mechanical conventions in written compositions

4. Gathers and uses information for research purposes

Standards for Writing
Grades 6-8

Level III (Grades 6–8)

1. Demonstrates competence in the general skills and strategies of the writing process

A. Prewriting: Uses a variety of prewriting strategies (e.g., makes outlines, uses published pieces as writing models, constructs critical standards, brainstorms, builds background knowledge)

B. Drafting and Revising: Uses a variety of strategies to draft and revise written work (e.g., analyzes and clarifies meaning, makes structural and syntactical changes, uses an organizational scheme, uses sensory words and figurative language, rethinks and rewrites for different audiences and purposes, checks for a consistent point of view and for transitions between paragraphs, uses direct feedback to review compositions)

C. Editing and Publishing: Uses a variety of strategies to edit and publish written work (e.g., eliminates slang; edits for grammar, punctuation, capitalization, and spelling at a developmentally appropriate level; proofreads using reference materials, word processor, and other resources; edits for clarity, word choice, and language usage; uses a word processor to publish written work)

D. Evaluates own and others' writing (e.g., applies criteria generated by self and others, uses self-assessment to set and achieve goals as a writer, participates in peer response groups)

E. Uses style and structure appropriate for specific audiences (e.g., public, private) and purposes (e.g., to entertain, to influence, to inform)

F. Writes expository compositions (e.g, presents information that reflects knowledge about the topic of the report; organizes and presents information in a logical manner)

G. Writes narrative accounts (e.g., engages the reader by establishing a context and otherwise developing reader interest; establishes a situation, plot, persona, point of view, setting, and conflict; creates an organizational structure that balances and unifies all narrative aspects of the story; uses sensory details and concrete language to develop plot and character; excludes extraneous details and inconsistencies; develops complex characters; uses a range of strategies such as dialogue, tension or suspense, naming a specific narrative action such as movement, gestures, and expressions)

H. Writes compositions about autobiographical incidents (e.g., explores the significance and personal importance of the incident; uses details to provide a context for the incident; reveals personal attitude towards the incident; presents details in a logical manner)

I. Writes biographical sketches (e.g., illustrates the subject's character using narrative and descriptive strategies such as relevant dialogue, specific action, physical description, background description, and comparison or contrast to other people; reveals the significance of the subject to the writer; presents details in a logical manner)

J. Writes persuasive compositions (e.g., engages the reader by establishing a context, creating a persona, and otherwise developing reader interest; develops a controlling idea that conveys a judgment; creates and organizes a structure appropriate to the needs and interests of a specific audience; arranges details, reasons, examples, and/or anecdotes persuasively; excludes information and arguments that are irrelevant; anticipates and addresses reader concerns and counter-arguments; supports arguments with detailed evidence, citing sources of information appropriately)

Standards for Writing *(cont.)*
Grades 6-8

K. Writes compositions that speculate on problems/solutions (e.g., identifies and defines a problem in a way appropriate to the intended audience, describes at least one solution, presents logical and well-supported reasons)

L. Writes in response to literature (e.g., anticipates and answers a reader's questions, responds to significant issues in a log or journal, answers discussion questions, writes a summary of a book, describes an initial impression of a text, connects knowledge from a text with personal knowledge)

M. Writes business letters and letters of request and response (e.g., uses business letter format; states purpose of the letter; relates opinions, problems, requests, or compliments; uses precise vocabulary)

2. Demonstrates competence in the stylistic and rhetorical aspects of writing

A. Uses descriptive language that clarifies and enhances ideas (e.g., establishes tone and mood, uses figurative language)

B. Uses paragraph form in writing (e.g., arranges sentences in sequential order, uses supporting and follow-up sentences)

C. Uses a variety of sentence structures to express expanded ideas

D. Uses some explicit transitional devices

3. Uses grammatical and mechanical conventions in written compositions

A. Uses simple and compound sentences in written compositions

B. Uses pronouns in written compositions (e.g., relative, demonstrative, personal [i.e., possessive, subject, object])

C. Uses nouns in written compositions (e.g, forms possessive of nouns, forms irregular plural nouns)

D. Uses verbs in written compositions (e.g., uses linking and auxiliary verbs, verb phrases, and correct forms of regular and irregular verbs)

E. Uses adjectives in written compositions (e.g., pronominal, positive, comparative, superlative)

F. Uses adverbs in written compositions (e.g., chooses between forms of adjectives and adverbs)

G. Uses prepositions and coordinating conjunctions in written compositions (e.g., uses prepositional phrases, combines and embeds ideas using conjunctions)

H. Uses interjections in written compositions

I. Uses conventions of spelling in written compositions (e.g., spells high frequency, commonly misspelled words from appropriate grade-level list, uses a dictionary and other resources to spell words, uses common prefixes and suffixes as aids to spelling, applies rules for irregular structural changes)

Standards for Writing *(cont.)*
Grades 6-8

J. Uses conventions of capitalization in written compositions (e.g., titles, [books, stories, poems, magazines, newspapers, songs, works of art], proper nouns [team names, companies, schools and institutions, departments of government, religions, school subject], proper adjectives, nationalities, brand names of products)

K. Uses conventions of punctuation in written compositions (e.g, uses exclamation marks after exclamatory sentences and interjections; uses periods in decimals, dollars, and cents; uses commas with nouns of address and after mild interjections; uses quotation marks with poems, songs, and chapters; uses colons in business letter salutations; uses hyphens to divide words between syllables at the end of a line)

L. Uses standard format in written compositions (e.g., includes footnotes, uses italics [for titles of books, magazines, plays, movies])

4. Gathers and uses information for research purposes

A. Gathers data for research topics from interviews (e.g., prepares and asks relevant questions, makes notes of responses, compiles responses)

B. Uses the card catalog to locate books for research topics

C. Uses the *Reader's Guide to Periodical Literature* and other indexes to gather information for research topics

D. Uses a computer catalog to gather information for research topics

E. Uses a variety of resource materials to gather information for research topics (e.g., magazines, newspapers, dictionaries, schedules, journals, phone directories, globes, atlases, almanacs)

F. Determines the appropriateness of an information source for a research topic

G. Organizes information and ideas from multiple sources in systematic ways (e.g., time lines, outlines, notes, graphic representations)

H. Writes research papers (e.g., separates information into major components based on a set of criteria, examines critical relationships between and among elements of a research topic, integrates a variety of information into a whole)

Student Survey

Directions: Read the following statements. Underneath each statement, circle the word(s) that most clearly reflects your opinion.

1. I enjoy reading poetry.

   strongly agree   agree   neutral   disagree   strongly disagree

2. I enjoy writing poetry.

   strongly agree   agree   neutral   disagree   strongly disagree

3. The best poems rhyme.

   strongly agree   agree   neutral   disagree   strongly disagree

4. Poetry is hard to understand.

   strongly agree   agree   neutral   disagree   strongly disagree

5. Writing poetry is difficult.

   strongly agree   agree   neutral   disagree   strongly disagree

6. Poems are boring.

   strongly agree   agree   neutral   disagree   strongly disagree

7. Poets usually use old-fashioned words in their poems.

   strongly agree   agree   neutral   disagree   strongly disagree

8. Poems are hard to punctuate.

   strongly agree   agree   neutral   disagree   strongly disagree

9. Poems are usually about boring subjects.

   strongly agree   agree   neutral   disagree   strongly disagree

10. The first word of every line in a poem needs to be capitalized.

    strongly agree   agree   neutral   disagree   strongly disagree

- -

Note: Fold on line before making copies for students.

Note to the teacher: You may wish to use this questionnaire as a pre- and post-assessment of students' attitudes toward poetry. Administer the questionnaire prior to beginning poetry instruction and after the completion of the unit. Discuss with students any differences in their answers between the first and last assessment.

What Is Poetry?

What is poetry? Famous poets have defined poetry in different ways. W. H. Auden calls it "memorable speech." Matthew Arnold sees poetry as "criticism of life." William Wordsworth believes poetry is "the spontaneous overflow of powerful feelings." What is your definition of poetry?

Generally, poets use language differently than prose writers. Poets choose a limited number of words for their poems, words that say exactly what the poet intends. Poets do not waste words; they use only the most powerful, precise words in their poems. Poetry often expresses a strong feeling or emotion. The poet's choice of words enhances the intended feeling or emotional content of the poem.

In the following haiku, the poet describes the sky as he sees it:

Blue sky up above
I see floating images
Cartoons in the clouds

The poet has used only twelve words but has conveyed his thoughts about gazing at the sky. His last line, "Cartoons in the clouds," paints a clear picture of his perception of the clouds. His use of alliteration—the repetition of the *c /k/* sound in the words *cartoons* and *clouds*—enhances the dreamy, light-hearted feeling of the poem by making the last line musical.

Poetry is usually written in verse. Groups of lines in a poem are called stanzas. Lines often have a definite rhythm, or beat. Sometimes poets create lines that rhyme:

Winter is so very nice
Ski, sled, and skate on ice.
I like it when the snow comes down
They close the schools all over town.
My friends and I go out to play
We hope for snow another day!

Sometimes lines don't rhyme:

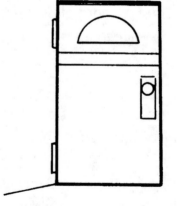

There he was
Alive, strong, and looking well.
I saw the happiness in his eyes,
In his laughter,
In his smile.
It looked like it would never fade.
As I stepped out of his door and said goodbye,
I didn't mean forever.

What Is Poetry? *(cont.)*

How do you feel after reading each of these two poems? Which one is intended to be a fun-loving, quick-reading poem? Which one is more serious? How would the serious poem change if the author had used rhyming lines?

Poets are usually more succinct than prose writers. That is, poets convey their messages with fewer words and in less space than do prose writers. Each word the poet uses, each writing technique the poet employs, each placement of a word on a line is done purposefully to achieve the desired effect on the reader. The change poem below illustrates such an effect.

Autumn Snow

Leaves
Fall
To the
Ground
And
Blanket
The
Earth
With
Snow
On
A
Mid
Winter's
Day.

Poets take great care to ensure that their poem expresses their intended message. As poet Samuel Coleridge defined it, poetry is "the best words in the best order."

As you read and write poetry, remember these definitions and ideas. Keep them in mind as you read to understand poetry and as you choose words and techniques when you write poetry. Keep them in mind and you will love poetry!

To become a poet:

1. Choose your words so that your reader will remember your poem. Remember, poetry is "memorable speech."

2. Choose a subject which has value, that makes a point. Remember, poetry is "criticism of life."

3. Write about a subject for which you have passion. Pour your emotions into the poem. Choose the precise words to express your emotion. Use words powerful enough to evoke a strong feeling from the reader. Remember, poetry is "the spontaneous overflow of powerful feelings."

4. Use your paper as if it were an artist's canvas. Choose words that create a picture in the reader's mind. Arrange the words in purposeful lines and stanzas. Use punctuation, capitalization, and white space as details that further enhance the image. Remember, poetry is "the best words in the best order."

Strategies for Reading and Understanding Poetry

Some poems may seem like a mystery to you. You might think, "I have no idea what this poem is about!" Others seem very simple, but may have a deeper meaning that you didn't realize on the first reading. Reading and understanding poetry becomes easier when you use the following strategy for reading poems:

Listen: Poetry often has a musical quality. Listen to the rhythm of the poem as you read it. Listen to the natural pauses created by line breaks and white space. Listen to who is speaking in the poem.

Look: Close your eyes and visualize the words of the poem. What images come to mind? What do you think the poet was seeing that prompted him or her to write the poem?

Feel: Think about how the poem makes you feel. What emotion or feeling is the poet trying to express? What is the tone of the poem?

Look again: Read each word one by one. Poems are often filled with language that says one thing but means another. As you read, stop to clarify. Ask yourself, "What does this word mean?" Are there any hidden meanings in the poem? Reread the title of the poem. What is the importance of the title?

Listen again: What is the poet saying? What is the message of the poem?

Strategies for Reading and Understanding Poetry *(cont.)*

Directions: Read the following poem. Apply the reading strategy below to help you understand the poem better.

His Story

History lacks herstory
    The essential fault is in
        The pronoun

Kings, lords, warriors and knights, even
    Explorers: all males
        (some wearing mail,
        some setting sail aboard ships named after females.)

His-story lacks her-story
    We-males need
    Fe-males.
    Prince Henry, Edward the First
    Alex the Great, Peter the Worst
        Where are the daughters?
        Do we ignore the wives?
    Just X's on record—
        So are there no Y's?

Please rewind
    research
    review
    And relearn

Both sides of OUR-story
    Give females their turn.

Listen: Listen to the rhythm of the poem as you read it.

Look: What images come to mind when you read this poem? _____

_____

Feel: How does the poem make you feel? _____

_____

Look again: Read each word one by one. Are there any hidden meanings? _____

What are they? _____

What is the importance of the title? _____

Listen again: What is the poet saying? What is the message? _____

_____

Definitions and Examples of Poetry Terms

alliteration: the repetition of beginning consonant sounds in words

    Example: *In the summer the sun is strong.*

assonance: the repetition of vowel sounds in words

    Examples: *paid, same, make, rain*

consonance: the repetition of consonant sounds anywhere in words

    Example: *Bring back the black jacket.*

couplet: a two-line stanza, usually rhymed

    Example: *When I was riding straight through the town,*

                The driving rain began to pour down.

diction: the writer's choice of words

end rhyme: the rhyming of words at the ends of two or more lines

    Example: *See couplet, above.*

figurative language: language that uses figures of speech and cannot be taken literally

formula poetry: poems that follow a specified formula or pattern

    Examples: *haiku, limerick, sonnet*

free verse: poems that can be written as the author chooses; they do not follow a specified rhyme scheme or pattern

hyperbole: an exaggeration that something either has much more or much less of a quality than it actually has

    Example: *He runs so fast he could catch a bullet.*

imagery: mental pictures that are created with words

    Example: *Soft snow falls steadily upon the waiting roofs*

                The fluffy flakes create a mound of white powder . . .

metaphor: a comparison of two things without using "like" or "as"

    Example: *Paul Bunyan is a mountain of a man.*

meter: the pattern of stressed and unstressed syllables in lines of poetry

    Example: *The long day wanes*

                the slow moon climbs

                the stars abound

                across the sky

mood: the emotion you feel when you read a poem

narrative: a poem that tells a story

onomatopoeia: the use of words that sound like the objects or actions they describe

    Example: *The boom of the thunder woke me from my nap.*

oxymoron: a phrase that combines two seemingly contradictory elements

    Examples: *icy hot; jumbo shrimp; bittersweet*

Definitions and Examples
of Poetry Terms *(cont.)*

personification: a description of non-human objects or ideas using human characteristics

    Example: *winter trees are starving, lacking leaves of spring*

poetry: words arranged in a rhythm that express ideas and emotions

pun: a play on words with similar sounds or on one word with multiple meanings

    Example: *That cowboy has galloped right out of my life,*

        Some say I gave him the boot . . .

repetition: the repeating of a word or phrase in a line or poem

    Example: *In my sleep, I dream*

        in my sleep, I believe

        in my sleep, I mourn

rhyme: when two or more words have the same sound

    Examples:

        single rhyme: *cat, hat*

        double rhyme: *napping, tapping*

        triple rhyme: *mournfully, scornfully*

        internal rhyme: *The cat sat happily purring.*

rhyme scheme: a pattern of accented and unaccented syllables

simile: a comparison of two things using "like" or "as"

    Example: *Paul Bunyan is as big as a mountain.*

stress: emphasis given to a word or syllable

stanza: a number of lines that divide a poem into sections

symbol: an object, person, action, or situation that signifies more than itself

    Example: Keep in mind that a dove is a symbol of peace as you read the following line of poetry:

    A single white dove flew above the warring country,

    lost in its path . . .

tone: the writer's attitude toward a subject

Poetry Resources

Cole, William. *Poet Stew.* Lippincott, 1981.

de Regniers, Beatrice Schenk. *The Way I Feel . . . Sometimes.* Clarion, 1988.

Dunning, Stephen. *Reflections on a Gift of Watermelon Pickle and Other Modern Verse.* Scholastic, 1966.

Field, Edward. *Magic Words.* Gulliver Books, 1998.

Frost, Robert. *You Come Too: Favorite Poems for Young Readers.* Scholastic, 1975.

Gaige, Amity. *We Are a Thunderstorm.* Landmark Editions, 1990. (This is an excellent book of poetry written by a 16-year-old student.)

Glenn, Mel. *Class Dismissed II: More High School Poems.* Clarion, 1986.

Hopkins, Lee Bennett. *Marvelous Math.* Simon and Schuster, 1997.

Janeczko, Paul B. *Poetspeak: in their work about their work.* Bradbury Press, 1983.

Koch, Kenneth. *Rose, Where Did You Get That Red? Teaching Great Poetry to Children.* Vintage Books, 1990.

Larrick, Nancy. *I Heard a Scream in the Street: Poetry by Young People in the City.* M. Evans and Co., 1970.

Lipson, Greta Barclay. *Audacious Poetry: Reflections of Adolescence.* Good Apple, 1992.

Molloy, Paul, ed. *Poetry U.S.A.* Scholastic, 1968.

Prelutsky, Jack. *The New Kid on the Block.* Greenwillow, 1984.

Prelutsky, Jack. *Something Big Has Been Here.* Greenwillow, 1990.

Romano, Tom. *Clearing the Way: Working with Teenage Writers.* Heinemann, 1987.

Sears, Peter. *Gonna Bake Me a Rainbow Poem: A Student Guide to Writing Poetry.* Scholastic, 1990.

Silverstein, Shel. *Falling Up.* HarperCollins, 1996.

Silverstein, Shel. *A Light In the Attic.* HarperCollins, 1981.

Silverstein, Shel. *Where the Sidewalk Ends.* HarperCollins, 1974.

Soto, Gary. *A Fire in My Hands: A Book of Poems.* Scholastic, 1990.

Swann, Brian. *Touching the Distance: Native American Riddle Poems.* Browndeer Press, 1998.

Turner, Ann. *Mississippi Mud.* HarperCollins, 1997.

Viorst, Judith. *If I Were in Charge of the World and Other Worries.* Atheneum, 1981.

Viorst, Judith. *Sad Underwear and Other Complications.* Atheneum, 1995.

Teacher's Guide to Generating Ideas for Writing

Picture File

Create a picture file that students can use as a stimulus for writing. Collect photos from calendars, magazines, or newspapers that might be intriguing enough to spark an idea in a student's mind. You may wish to mount the photos on construction paper or poster board and laminate them for durability. Keep the pictures in a crate or box in your classroom for easy student access. You may even wish to have students create a personal picture file as a long-term homework assignment.

Interest Inventory

Since the subject students know best is themselves, instruct students to complete the Interest Inventory on page 19 to generate ideas for possible poetry subjects. Keep the students' inventories in a binder that students can access when they are stuck for ideas, or have the students keep their own inventories for quick reference.

Idea Center

Designate an area of your classroom as the "Idea Center." Allow students to visit this center when they need ideas for writing. Stock it with all kinds of miscellaneous material that may spark students' creativity: baby name books, encyclopedias, rhyming dictionaries, newspapers, magazines, maps, atlases, artwork, cassette tapes and headphones, ads, fliers, phone books—the possibilities are endless. You never know where a student might get an idea for writing.

Poetry Library

Purchase or borrow several poetry collections and make them available to students to read as often as possible. You may even wish to include poems written by your students. Reading other poets' work is the best way to help students grow as poets themselves.

Prop Box

Select a fairly large box with a lid (the boxes that hold reams of copy paper work well). Cover the box and lid with contact paper to give it an attractive appearance. Fill the box with miscellaneous items: a running shoe, sunglasses, a fur stole, a gold-beaded purse, an empty stick of deodorant, an umbrella, an empty bottle of sunscreen, a box of tissues, a belt—the more off-beat, the better. Allow students to pick an item from the box and use that as the subject for a poem such as an ode or character poem.

Teacher's Guide to Generating Ideas for Writing *(cont.)*

Word Wheels

Obtain two cardboard pizza wheels from a local pizza store or cut two large circles out of cardboard. Using markers, divide the wheels into eight pie-shaped slices. On one wheel, write a different adjective in each slice. On the other wheel, write a different noun in each slice. Using a large metal brad, connect a cardboard arrow to the center of each wheel. Students can spin the arrows on each wheel and put the selected words together to obtain a subject for a poem such as "slimy shoes," "frozen heart," or "blue summer."

Word Log

Ask students to maintain logs of words that strike them as interesting or unusual. Depending on the word, they may wish to jot down the definition or the context in which the word was used. They should keep a running list as they read poems or prose or hear words in conversation. The log will help them remember those words when they are searching for just the right one for their poems.

Subject Bulletin Board

Design a bulletin board to help students select subjects for their poems. Collect 26 envelopes or small boxes (clean French fry containers work well). Print a letter of the alphabet on each of the containers. In each envelope or box, place several strips of paper printed with words beginning with that letter of the alphabet. For example, "A" could contain strips that say the following: aardvark, animal sounds, action figures, amusement parks, avalanches, Australia, etc. Students can pick a strip from any of the containers and use the word or phrase as a subject for a poem. The title of your board could be "Poetry Is as Easy as ABC!" Students could even create this bulletin board as a class project in preparation for starting the poetry lessons.

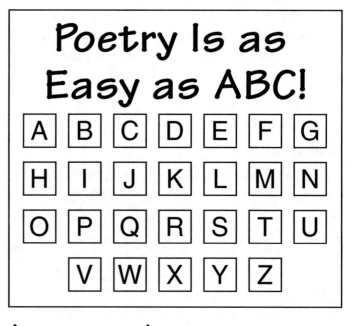

Inspirational Scrapbook

Instruct students to keep a scrapbook and fill it with thoughts, feelings, images, memorabilia, anything that strikes them as personal, or important. They could record their feelings in writing or include actual items that generate a memory or emotion. Students could refer to their scrapbook to discover ideas for poems with a personal touch.

Interest Inventory

Directions: Complete this interest inventory as specifically and completely as possible. This information is for your use; it will not be shared with anyone else. You will be able to use this information to generate ideas for poems that you are going to write. The more information you include on this sheet, the easier it will be to think of poetry ideas.

What are your hobbies? _____

_____

What is something unique about you? _____

_____

What do you love? _____

_____

What do you hate? _____

_____

What makes you cry? _____

_____

What makes you queasy? _____

_____

What makes you worried? _____

_____

What one thing do you wish you could change about yourself? _____

_____

What do you like best about yourself? _____

_____

Of what are you afraid? _____

_____

What superstitions do you have? _____

_____

What career do you want to pursue? _____

_____

What do you know about that some other people don't? _____

_____

What is your proudest moment? _____

_____

What is your most embarrassing moment? _____

_____

What is the saddest thing that ever happened to you? _____

_____

What is the funniest thing that you ever saw? _____

_____

Skill Using Rhyme

Background for the Teacher

Definition: *Rhyme* occurs when two or more words have the same sound. Rhyming words generally give poems a light-hearted quality. A rhyme scheme is the pattern of rhyme in a stanza or poem.

Materials Needed: Rhyme Time work sheet (page 21), Rhyming Words Grouping Strips (page 22)

Preparation: Make one copy of Rhyming Words Grouping Strips. Cut the strips apart. Place the strips in an envelope for storage until the lesson. Duplicate Rhyme Time work sheets for each student in the class.

Lesson Plan

1. Divide students into groups of three by distributing the grouping strips at the beginning of the lesson. Instruct students to locate their group by finding other students who have words that rhyme with the word on their own strips of paper. Students should sit with their group members when they have located everyone.

2. Inform the students that they will be playing a game called "Rhyme Time." Explain the rules of the game to the students as follows:

   > Each team will designate one student to be a recorder. The teacher will call out a word. All teams will have two minutes to brainstorm as many words as they can think of that rhyme with the word the teacher said. (Remind students that the words should be actual words, not non-sensical ones.) The recorder for each group will write down the words. At the end of two minutes, the teacher will call time and students are to stop writing. The teacher will lead the groups in sharing their lists of rhyming words. If groups thought of the same word, the word gets crossed off from everyone's list. Groups earn points for brainstorming unique words that no other group has on their list.

3. After students have had ample practice generating single rhyming words, present the concept of rhyme scheme. Inform students that a rhyme scheme is a pattern of rhyme in a stanza or poem.

4. Distribute Rhyme Time work sheets. Review the directions with students. Instruct the students to complete the work sheet in order to practice identifying rhyme schemes.

Rhyme Time

Directions: A rhyme scheme is a pattern of rhyme in a stanza or poem. Identify the rhyme schemes in the following stanzas by first underlining the end rhymes and then assigning letters to the rhyming words. An example has been done for you.

Like the sun behind the _clouds_   A

Like the darkness of the _night_   B

Like the grass beneath the _trees_   C

You stepped into the _light_ . . .   B

I knew I'd have to grow up sometime,   _____

That my childhood memories would end,   _____

But a spark within me died,   _____

When I lost my imaginary friend.   _____

As the sun set and the moon came,   _____

I looked out the window in dread and shame.   _____

The sound of birds rose from the sky,   _____

I waved my hand and bid goodbye.   _____

When I look into his eyes,   _____

I see the deep blue sea.   _____

I hope my love never dies,   _____

That he'll always be there for me.   _____

And here ends the saga,   _____

Of writers who have grown.   _____

We're successful authors,   _____

Now we will be known.   _____

Rhyming Words Grouping Strips

Directions: This sheet has sets of rhyming words. You will need to calculate how many copies you need to make in order to put your students in small groups. Once you have made copies, cut apart the strips and distribute a word to each student. Students must find other students whose word rhymes with the one printed on their own strip.

rain	train	brain
hat	cat	sat
four	pour	more
book	look	took
bend	mend	send
moan	alone	phone
greet	retreat	meet
will	still	bill
floor	store	door

Using Assonance and Consonance

Background for the Teacher

Definition: *Assonance* is the repetition of vowel sounds anywhere in words; *consonance* is the repetition of consonant sounds anywhere in the words.

Materials Needed: Sounds the Same work sheet (page 24)

Preparation: Reproduce one Sounds the Same work sheet for each group of 3 or 4 students in your class.

Lesson Plan

1. Define assonance and consonance for students.

2. Inform students that these are techniques poets use to enhance the effect of their poetry. Assonance and consonance help create a light hearted, fun, musical quality in poems.

3. Create groups of 3 or 4 students each.

4. Distribute the Sounds the Same work sheet. Assist students in identifying the assonance and consonance in the sample provided. Review the directions with students.

5. When students have completed the work sheet, allow groups to share their lines of poetry. Identify whether assonance or consonance was used.

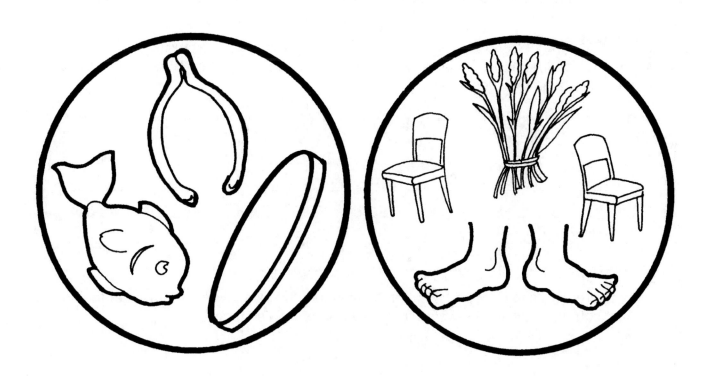

Sounds the Same

Assonance is the repetition of vowel sounds in a line of poetry. The following line contains an example of assonance:

I *paid* my *way* on the *plane* to *Maine*.

The long a sound is repeated in the words *paid, way, plane,* and *Maine.*

Consonance is the repetition of consonant sounds in a line of poetry. The line below contains consonance, in which the *b* and *ck* consonant sounds are repeated.

Bring back the *black jacket*.

Using Assonance

Brainstorm words that have the following vowel sounds. Some examples have been provided.

a	e	i	o	u
rain	wheat	light	goat	hue
_____	_____	_____	_____	_____
_____	_____	_____	_____	_____
_____	_____	_____	_____	_____
_____	_____	_____	_____	_____
_____	_____	_____	_____	_____

Now try to create a line of poetry that has assonance using words that repeat the same vowel sound. You can use words from any one of the lists above.

Using Consonance

Brainstorm words that have the same sound as the consonant combinations below. Some examples have been provided.

ck	dge	ch	sh	br	wh
black	fudge	cheek	wish	broken	whirl
_____	_____	_____	_____	_____	_____
_____	_____	_____	_____	_____	_____
_____	_____	_____	_____	_____	_____
_____	_____	_____	_____	_____	_____
_____	_____	_____	_____	_____	_____

Now, try to create a line of poetry that has consonance by using words that repeat the same consonant sound. You can use words from any one of the lists above.

Using Rhythm

Background for the Teacher

Definition: *Rhythm* is a regular pattern of accented and unaccented syllables in lines of poetry.

Materials Needed: rhythm sticks or pencils, two for each student; a copy of a favorite poem, preferably one that has a distinct rhythm

Preparation: Gather the materials needed for the lesson.

Lesson Plan

1. Clap your hands loudly in a rhythmic pattern to gain the attention of the class. Clap your hands again using the same rhythm, then instruct students to clap back the same rhythm.

2. Repeat this exercise several times with different rhythms.

3. Have the students pair up. Distribute the rhythm sticks or the pencils to students (each student will need two).

4. Instruct the pairs of students to continue the same activity on their own, with one partner establishing a rhythm and playing it on their pencils or rhythm sticks, and the other partner echoing the pattern in answer.

5. After sufficient practice, collect the rhythm sticks or pencils from the students.

6. In the same manner as the previous activity, recite a line from a poem, using inflection in your voice as you speak. Instruct students to repeat the same line, using the same inflection you used.

7. Continue with this exercise, instructing students to pay particular attention to the words you accent and don't accent. Explain that this pattern of accented and unaccented syllables is creating the rhythm of the line.

8. Finally, vocalize the rhythm in the first line of "There was an old woman who lived in a shoe," using only the sounds "Da dá da da dá da da dá da da dá." Instruct students to mimic the rhythm using the same sound. Then, instruct students to compose a line of poetry (using any words they wish) that fits the same rhythm, for example, "My mother can help me to water the plants."

9. Provide further practice using rhythm as needed.

Using Alliteration

Background for the Teacher

Definition: *Alliteration* is the repetition of beginning consonant sounds in words.

Materials Needed: Alliteration Action work sheet (page 27); highlighters, colored pencils, or markers for each student

Preparation: Reproduce one Alliteration Action work sheet for each student.

Lesson Plan

1. Write the following tongue twisters on the chalkboard:

    > *Betty bought a batch of buns at the bakery.*
    > *Sammy swam, sat, and sang, all by the seashore.*
    > *Large Larry Lewis lounges at the lake.*

2. Call on several students to try to say the tongue twisters as quickly as they can. Let students have fun with this! Ask students what makes tongue twisters so difficult to say. Hopefully, they will recognize that the repetition of the same consonant sound makes it difficult to pronounce the words quickly.

3. Define *alliteration* for students. Point out the alliteration in each of the tongue twisters from #1, above.

4. Explain that *alliteration* is a technique poets sometimes use to make their poems catchy or interesting to the reader.

5. Distribute the Alliteration Action work sheets. Two more tongue twisters are provided for students to try to pronounce in the first section of the work sheet. Using a highlighter, colored pencil, or marker, have students highlight the initial consonant sound in each of the words of the tongue twisters.

6. Allow students to complete the second section of the work sheet independently, underlining the alliterative consonants in the three examples provided.

7. Depending on the skill level of your students, have students complete the third section of alliterative lines independently or with a partner. Check their completed lines for accuracy.

8. Provide extra practice in alliteration as needed.

Alliteration Action

Alliteration is a poetic technique in which the beginning consonant sound is repeated in words for effect. Tongue twisters often use alliteration to create catchy phrases. Notice the effect of alliteration as you try to say the following tongue twisters:

Six silly sailors swam south.
Bobby bought a bunch of brown bananas.

Alliteration Practice

Underline the alliterative consonants in the following sentences.

Example: Snakes slither on the sidewalk.

1. The wind whistled through the willows.

2. Magic markers can make masterpieces.

3. Tommy tried to twist, but tumbled.

4. Greg grabbed the garnish from the graceful bowl.

5. Constance catered to her cat with catnip to keep it from kidnapping canaries.

Use alliteration to finish the lines below.

1. People patiently _____

2. Roger ran _____

3. Six swimmers _____

4. Alan always _____

5. Kelly caught _____

Now, write five alliterative sentences of your own.

1. _____

2. _____

3. _____

4. _____

5. _____

Using Onomatopoeia

Background for the Teacher

Definition: *Onomatopoeia* uses words that sound like the objects or actions which they are describing.

Materials Needed: What's That Sound? (page 29) and Onomatopoeic Words (page 30) work sheet

Preparation: Reproduce one What's That Sound? and Onomatopoeic Words work sheet for each student.

Lesson Plan

1. Define *onomatopoeia* for students.

2. Distribute the What's That Sound? work sheet. Review the directions on the work sheet and complete the first part of the work sheet with the students. Help students notice that the sounds that animals make are examples of onomatopoeia.

3. Continue pointing out examples of onomatopoeia by completing the second section of the work sheet, writing sounds that specific objects make.

4. To complete the work sheet, assist students in generating sounds that would be heard if they were involved in the actions listed in the third section of the work sheet.

5. Hand out the Onomatopeic Words work sheets to students to use as a reference for poetry writing.

What's That Sound?

What sound does each of the following animals make?

a cat _____

a duck _____

a dog _____

a sheep _____

a horse _____

a snake _____

What sound does each of the following objects make?

a train _____

the ocean _____

a balloon _____

a door _____

the wind _____

thunder _____

What sounds would you hear if you were . . .

at a football game? _____

trick-or-treating? _____

bowling? _____

toasting a piece of bread? _____

blowing a bubble with bubble gum? _____

emptying a dishwasher? _____

listening to a thunderstorm? _____

watching fireworks? _____

waking up? _____

running to answer a ringing phone? _____

hitting a home run? _____

Onomatopoeic Words

Use the following list to help you use onomatopoeic words in your poems.

- bang
- beep
- blink
- boom
- bow wow
- buzz
- chirp
- chug
- clang
- clap
- clatter
- click
- cluck
- cough
- crack
- crackle
- crash
- creak
- crunch
- cuckoo
- ding dong
- drip
- fizz
- flip flop
- glug
- grate
- grind
- gurgle
- hiss
- honk
- hum
- meow
- moan
- moo

- muffle
- munch
- murmur
- muzzle
- ping
- plop
- quack
- rattle
- ring
- rip
- roar
- rustle
- shuffle
- sizzle
- slam
- slap
- slurp
- smack
- snag
- snap
- splash
- squeak
- squeal
- squish
- swish
- tap
- thump
- tic tock
- warble
- whack
- whisk
- whisper
- yawn
- zoom

Using Similes

Background for the Teacher

Definition: A *simile* is a technique for comparing two things using the words *like* or *as*.

Materials Needed: Similarities work sheet (page 32)

Preparation: Reproduce one Similarities work sheet for each student in the class.

Lesson Plan

1. Write the words *eyes* and *diamonds* on the chalkboard.

2. Ask students to explain how *eyes* and *diamonds* might be similar. (They will probably say that both eyes and diamonds can sparkle.)

3. On the board write the statement: *Her eyes were like diamonds.* Explain to students that this is an example of a simile. Define simile as a comparison using the words *like* or *as*.

4. Write two more words on the board: *grass* and *shirt*.

5. Ask students again how the words *grass* and *shirt* could be similar. Once the students arrive at the correct conclusion write this sentence on the board: *His shirt was as green as grass.*

6. Distribute the Similarities work sheet. Review the definition of a simile with students again. Instruct students to complete the work sheet independently to gain more practice with writing similes.

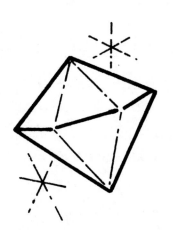

Her eyes were like diamonds.

Similarities

A *simile* is a technique for comparing two things. Similes use the words *like* or *as* to show how the items are alike. Here are some similes.

> *Her teeth are as white as winter snow.*
> (Her teeth are white and snow is white.)

> *The snake was like a garden hose.*
> (The snake was thin and black and lying in the grass. The garden hose was also thin and black and lying in the grass.)

Explain the comparisons in the following similes:

1. The baby's cheeks are like a rose.

   The baby's cheeks are _____ and a rose is _____.

2. The full moon is like a cookie.

   The full moon is _____ and a cookie is _____.

3. The baseball whizzed by like a bullet.

   The baseball is _____ and a bullet is _____.

4. The coffee is like ink.

   Coffee is _____ and ink is _____.

Now you try it. Write some similes of your own.

1. The boat is _____
   _____.

2. The cave is _____
   _____.

3. Her hair is _____
   _____.

Read your similes to a friend. See if he or she can explain your comparison.

Using Metaphors

Background for the Teacher

Definition: A *metaphor* is a technique for comparing two things. Unlike a simile, a metaphor does not use the words *like* or *as*.

Materials Needed: Love-ly Lines work sheet (page 34)

Preparation: Reproduce Love-ly Lines work sheet for each student.

Lesson Plan

1. Write the words *alarm clock* and *rooster* on the chalkboard.

2. Ask students to explain how an alarm clock and a rooster might be similar. (They will probably say that an alarm clock wakes a person up in the morning, just like a rooster does when it crows.)

3. On the board write the statement: *My alarm clock is a rooster.* Explain to students that this is an example of a metaphor. Define metaphor as a comparison that does not use the words *like* or *as*.

4. Expand the comparison by writing, *My alarm clock is a rooster, waking me at dawn's first light.* Explain that the elaboration helps the comparison make better sense to the reader.

5. Distribute the Love-ly Lines work sheet. Review the definition of a metaphor with students again. Instruct students to complete the work sheet independently, gaining more practice with writing metaphors.

Love-ly Lines

Love is a teddy bear, keeping me warm at night.

Love is a mountain, making me feel like I can touch the sky.

Love is a milkshake; sometimes you need to shake it up a little.

These lines use metaphors to describe love. The writer compares love to something, and then explains the connection. The comparison is called a *metaphor*. The writer is comparing two objects, but without using the words *like* or *as*, as are used in a simile.

See if you can explain the connection in the following metaphors.

1. Love is the wind,_____

   _____

2. Love is a rainbow,_____

   _____

3. Love is a sail on a sailboat, _____

   _____

Now try to write some metaphors along with explanations that help the reader better understand your meaning.

1. Time is _____

   _____.

2. Friendship is _____

   _____.

3. Anger is _____

   _____.

Using Repetition

Background for the Teacher

Definition: *Repetition* is the repeating of a word or a phrase in a line or a poem.

Materials Needed: My Life Line work sheet (page 36)

Preparation: Reproduce one My Life Line work sheet for each student in the class.

Lesson Plan

1. Read the following poem to the students:

   When I'm gone
   Gather my friends and celebrate my life
   For it was lived in peace.
   When I'm gone
   Scatter my ashes across the plains
   The land from which I came,
   Then plant a single flower
   In the hot desert sun
   And notice how beautiful it looks
   All alone
   Until it's gone.

2. Point out the repetition of the line "When I'm gone." Ask students what effect this repetition had on the tone of the poem.

3. Point out the twist in the repeated line at the end. It has changed to say "Until it's gone." Ask students why they think the author chose to change the repetition. What effect does it have on the poem's meaning?

4. Instruct students to create a time line of their lives by completing the My Life Line work sheet. Allow ample time for students to complete this activity.

5. Assist students in drafting a poem about their lives that uses repetition. Write the following line on the chalkboard:

   But time marches on.

6. Model for students the beginning of a poem using this line in repetition. You could use this example or create one specifically about you:

   I was born in a small country town;
   Everyone knew me the minute I arrived.
   There were only 400 of us in that town,
   But time marches on.

7. Instruct students to begin a poem about their life using an early event for the first stanza. The last line of the stanza should be "But time marches on."

8. Direct students to continue in this fashion, writing about each event in chronological order and ending with the repeated line.

9. When students near the end of their poems, challenge them to twist the repeated line to add interest to the ending.

10. Allow students to share their drafts if they choose.

My Life Line

Directions: Create a time line of major events in your life. Start with your birth. You could include birthdays, milestones such as losing teeth, sporting events or activities in which you participated, school events—anything that is important to you. Be sure to record the approximate year the event occurred.

Year:

Event:

Using Tone and Mood

Background for the Teacher

Definition: *Tone* is the writer's attitude toward a subject. *Mood* is the emotion a reader feels when reading a poem.

Materials Needed: Real Estate Wrap-Up work sheets (page 38–39)

Preparation: Reproduce one Real Estate Wrap-Up work sheets for each student in the class.

Lesson Plan

1. Write the following sentence on the chalkboard: *You're right.*

2. Ask student volunteers to say that sentence in the following manners:

   - with sarcasm
   - with surprise
   - with sadness
   - with honesty
   - with anger

3. Explain to students that each time one of the volunteers spoke, he or she was portraying a different tone. Define *tone* for students as the speaker's attitude toward a subject. When discussing poetry, tone is the poet's attitude toward a subject.

4. Explain that authors can create a certain tone by choosing appropriate words.

5. Ask students to write one sentence describing a small child as if the child were . . .

   - charming
   - brilliant
   - a nuisance
   - pathetic

6. Have students share their sentences. Ask the class to point out specific words that added to the tone of the sentence.

7. Inform students that authors can also create a mood in their reader by choosing appropriate words. Define *mood* as the emotion a reader feels when reading a poem.

8. Read the following excerpt to students. Ask them to identify its mood.

   > *The moss covered trees beckoned to me,*
   > *Closer and closer I crept.*
   > *The black night was closing in*
   > *A shrill shriek pierced the night,*
   > *A bone-chilling fear drove through my spine . . .*

9. Have students identify specific words that helped create the mood.

10. Distribute the Real Estate Wrap-Up work sheets. Review directions with students. When students have completed the work sheet, allow them to share their descriptions in small groups or with the entire class. Discuss the different tones and moods of the descriptions.

Real Estate Wrap-Up

Directions:

You have been asked to write a description of four different houses for a real estate magazine. Your job is to describe the houses accurately so that the potential buyers will know exactly what each house is like. Write a paragraph describing each of the houses listed below. You will have to use your imagination to create a picture of the house in your mind before you write. Remember, you are the writer—you set the tone and the mood of the description.

An Abandoned House

_____

_____

_____

_____

_____

_____

_____

_____

_____

❖   ❖   ❖

A Doll House

_____

_____

_____

_____

_____

_____

_____

_____

_____

_____

Real Estate Wrap-Up *(cont.)*

A Haunted House

_____

_____

_____

_____

_____

_____

_____

_____

_____

_____

❖   ❖   ❖

Your House

_____

_____

_____

_____

_____

_____

_____

_____

_____

_____

Using Persona

Background for the Teacher

Definition: The *persona* is the speaker of the poem. The speaker may or may not be the author. In this lesson, students will learn to use a persona other than themselves when writing.

Materials Needed: *The True Story of the Three Little Pigs* by Jon Scieszka (Viking Kestrel, 1989), Who Said That? work sheet (page 41)

Preparation: Obtain a copy of *The True Story of the Three Little Pigs* from your local library or bookstore. Reproduce one copy of the Who Said That? work sheet for each student in the class.

Lesson Plan

1. Instruct students to work with a partner and retell the story of the "Three Little Pigs." Most students will be familiar with this story and can easily retell it.

2. Ask students to think about the point of view of the story. Who is made out to be the "bad guy"? (The wolf.) For whom does the reader feel sympathy? (The pigs.)

3. Explain to students that there is another side of the story. Read *The True Story of the Three Little Pigs*. (This book tells the story from the wolf's point of view.)

4. As a class, draft a poem from the wolf's point of view that briefly tells his side of the story. You could start with:

    Let me tell you a story about three little pigs.
    They built these houses that weren't too big . . .

5. Read your finished poem. Don't worry about it being a perfected poem—the idea is just to let the wolf's side of the story be heard.

6. Explain to students that *persona* means the speaker of the poem. Ask them who the persona is in the poem you created together. (The wolf.)

7. For more practice, distribute the Who Said That? work sheet. Review the directions with students.

Answers for page 41:

1. a rooster

2. a cat

3. a husband or a father who is getting ready to die

4. a car

5. a homeless person

Who Said That?

Directions: The *persona* of a poem is the speaker of the poem. Read the following excerpts from poems and determine the persona.

1. My job in the morning is an easy one

   I crow and squawk and cock-a-doodle-do.

   The farmer jumps right out of bed . . .

   The persona is _____

2. I have but eight lives left to live

   I lost one late last night.

   My owner left the door ajar

   And I quickly took my flight . . .

   The persona is _____

3. I do not fear death

   It greets us all

   It will soon be my time to go

   I want to say goodbye, though, first

   To my family, my friends, my wife . . .

   The persona is _____

4. Vroom, vroom

   My engines rev.

   My driver takes the wheel . . .

   The persona is _____

5. It's horrible the way we live each day

   When we have to eat what you throw away.

   You live in a house, we live on the street

   In a cardboard box, do you think it has heat?

   The persona is _____

Using Precise Words

Background for the Teacher

Definition: Using *precise words* takes the ability to select the best word available to portray a feeling, image, or meaning.

Materials Needed: Making Lightning! work sheet (page 43)

Preparation: Reproduce one Making Lightning! work sheet for each student in the class.

Lesson Plan

1. Write the following quote from Mark Twain on the overhead or chalkboard:

   The difference between the right word and the almost right word is the difference between lightning and the lightning bug.

   Ask students to explain what the quote means. Ask students which is more powerful—lightning or a lightning bug. Ask students which Twain is saying is more powerful—the right word or the almost right word.

2. To illustrate the fact that words have shades of meaning and different words are appropriate for different situations, recruit some dramatic student volunteers. Tell the class that these students will be walking across the front of the room. Whisper to one of the students the instruction, "Gallop." This student should gallop across the front of the room. Whisper to the three other student volunteers the following instructions: strut, slink, stagger. After each performer has finished, ask the class to guess the exact word to describe the way the student was walking across the room. Point out that each of these students traveled in a different manner just as each of the words have different meanings and would be appropriate in different contexts. When writing, authors choose specific words in order to portray a tone or create a mood.

3. You could repeat the same exercise by asking students to say the word "no" as a bellow, a whisper, a protest, and a question. Again, elicit the shades of meaning for these words.

4. Inform students that specific, precise words such as these make writing more powerful.

5. Distribute the Making Lightning! work sheets. Review the directions with students. Instruct students to complete the work sheet to gain practice in choosing precise, descriptive words.

Making Lightning!

Directions: Listed below are some trite, non-descriptive words or phrases. Use your skill in selecting precise words to make the following more concrete, specific, and interesting.

Instead of . . .	Try
Black bird	**The jet-black darkness flew past my window.**
A flower	_____
The ocean	_____
A pretty girl	_____
A good cookie	_____
A shirt	_____
The girl laughed	_____
A strong smell	_____
Hot pizza	_____
Fast car	_____
Warm bed	_____
Rocky mountain	_____
Little boy	_____
An athlete	_____
An empty street	_____
My friend	_____
A teddy bear	_____

Using Imagery

Background for the Teacher

Definition: *Imagery* is the use of words to create pictures in a reader's mind.

Materials Needed: Just Imagine work sheet (page 45), crayons or colored pencils

Preparation: Reproduce one Just Imagine work sheet for each student in the class. Gather together the crayons or colored pencils for student use.

Lesson Plan

1. Write the following on the chalkboard: *Show, don't tell.*

2. Tell students that they are going to play a new game, not Show and Tell as they know it, but "Show, Don't Tell."

3. Write the following sentences on the chalkboard:

   The baseball player argued with the umpire.

   The ace pitcher hurled his glove at the mound, then spit words at the man behind the plate.

4. Ask students to identify which sentence tells what happened and which sentence shows what happened. (The second sentence is the better sentence—it shows what happened.)

5. Explain that writers use precise words to paint pictures in the reader's mind. This is how authors show the reader what is happening. It is much more exciting and interesting for the reader to be able to "see" in their mind what the author is writing about.

6. Challenge pairs of students to turn the following sentences into showing sentences:

   • The basement floor was flooded.
   • The toddler was angry.
   • The cars crashed.
   • I ate the chocolate doughnut.
   • The painting was an antique.

7. Allow students to share their showing sentences. Ask the class to point out specific words that helped paint a picture in their minds.

8. Distribute the Just Imagine work sheet. Review the directions with students. Read the poem "Mabel" aloud as students underline precise words. Allow time for students to complete the rest of the work sheet and share their original "Mabel" poems.

Just Imagine

Directions: Read the following poem. Underline precise words that help paint a picture of the subject in your mind. Then draw a picture of Mabel in the box below as she is described in the poem.

Mabel

At noon, Mabel emerged,

Glancing out the front door.

She was a glamorous, long-legged woman

In her early twenties.

Her skin, a pale alabaster silk,

Radiated with anticipation.

Her soft, periwinkle eyes sparkled

A secret that few knew.

Her fluffy red hair flowed in waves,

Framing the award-winning face,

The face that, without the Cover Girl,

The Maybelline, the Revlon,

Would never have won the

Model-of-the-Year Award.

Just Imagine *(cont.)*

In the poem *Mabel*, the author hints at the possibility that Mabel is not very attractive without a lot of cosmetics. How do you suppose Mabel looks without makeup?

Write a phrase to describe her overall appearance. _____

_____

Write a phrase to describe her skin. _____

_____

Write a phrase to describe her eyes. _____

_____

Write a phrase to describe her hair. _____

_____

Now, create your own poem about Mabel, portraying her as she would appear without makeup. Remember to use precise words to create an image in the reader's mind.

_____

_____

_____

_____

_____

_____

_____

_____

_____

_____

_____

_____

_____

_____

_____

_____

_____

Using Personification

Background for the Teacher

Definition: *Personification* gives human qualities to non-human ideas or objects.

Materials Needed: Personification Wheels Suggestions (page 48), tag board or cardboard pizza wheels, two brads, two paper arrows to fit tag board or cardboard pizza wheels

Preparation: Create personification wheels by cutting two circles from tag board or cardboard pizza wheels. Divide the wheels into sections as shown on page 48. Write one noun in each section on the noun wheel, one verb in each section on the verb wheel. Use a large metal brad through the center of each wheel to attach an arrow.

Lesson Plan

1. Read the following poem to students:

    > *The snow whispers to me a faint goodbye*
    > *And promises to return*
    > *After the seasons have run their course*
    > *And winter reigns supreme again.*

2. Ask students the following:

    - What is the snow doing in this poem? (*whispering*)
    - What else does the snow do? (*promises to return*)
    - What will the seasons do? (*run their course*)
    - What will winter do? (*reign supreme*)

3. Ask students if they think these subjects can really do these actions. (They should answer no.) Follow up by asking students why they think the author used this technique in the poem. What do these actions—promises, reigns, and so forth—mean in the poem?

4. Define *personification* for the students as giving human qualities to non-human objects or ideas.

5. Share the personification wheels with students. Show them how to spin one wheel to select a noun and the other wheel to select a verb. Select one noun and one verb to use as a class model, such as *wind* and *warns*.

6. Ask students to elaborate on the noun/verb combination by explaining why or how the noun does its action. Might the wind warn about a coming storm? Would it wail or moan?

7. Provide students with an opportunity to spin the personification wheels to create their own combinations for elaboration and possible use in a poem.

Personification Wheels Suggestions

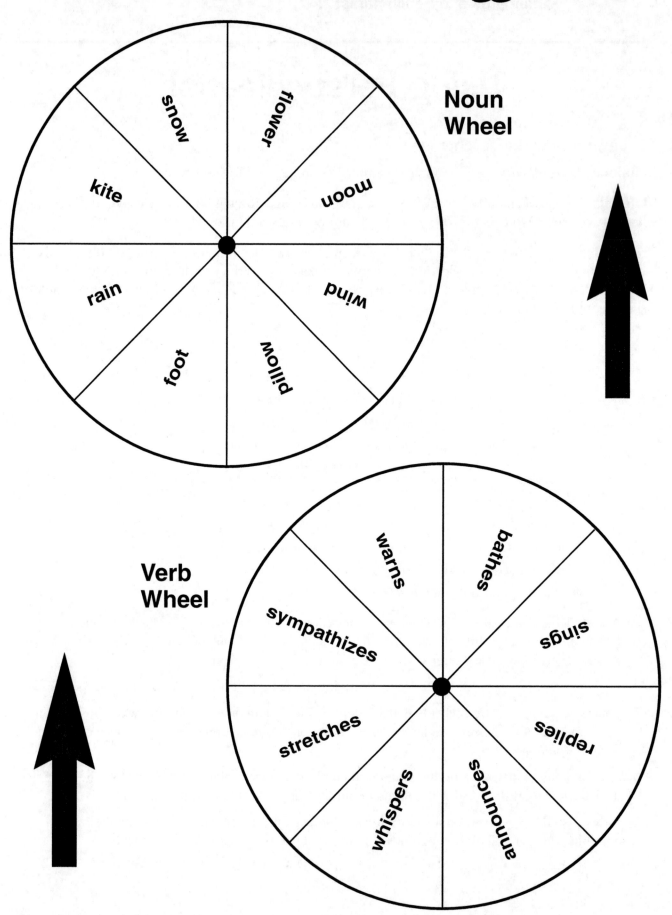

Noun Wheel

- snow
- flower
- kite
- moon
- rain
- wind
- foot
- pillow

Verb Wheel

- warns
- bathes
- sympathizes
- sings
- stretches
- replies
- whispers
- announces

Using Line Breaks and White Space

Background for the Teacher

Definition: Students will learn to arrange words into a poem, deliberately attending to *white space* on the paper and finding appropriate places to *break lines*. The lesson is particularly helpful for those students who just can't seem to write poetry that doesn't rhyme. This skill helps them understand how to break lines so that ideas written in prose turn into a poem quite easily.

Materials Needed: Line Breaks and White Space work sheet (page 52)

Preparation: Reproduce one copy of the Line Breaks and White Space work sheet for each student in the class.

Lesson Plan

1. Use a whole class round robin technique to generate a list of nouns. Going around the room, have students state a noun to be added to the class list you are creating. Encourage students to think of specific and unusual nouns.

2. Once you have a sufficient list, ask students to choose one of the nouns to use as a subject in a sentence.

3. Instruct students to write a sentence that contains exactly eight words—no more, no less!

4. Place the following poetry templates on the chalkboard:

Template 1

_____

_____   _____   _____

_____   _____

_____   _____

Template 2

_____   _____   _____

_____   _____   _____

_____

_____

Template 3

_____

_____   _____

_____

_____   _____

_____

_____

Line Breaks and White Space *(cont.)*

5. Have students rewrite their sentences in several different ways. Instruct them to use each of the templates on the board, placing one word on each line while using the same word order they created for their sentences. When students are finished, they will have rewritten their sentence in three different poem patterns. Allow students to create other patterns in which to write their sentences if time allows.

6. Ask students to read each of the pattern poems aloud to a partner. Have them notice if the different patterns make the sentence sound different. (Most likely students will pause at appropriate times as they read the sentence in the different poem forms.)

7. Explain to students that creating a poem can be simple. Authors can take sentences or paragraphs, and, by breaking them into phrases and lines at natural pauses, create a poem.

8. Repeat the same process by generating a class list of adjectives.

9. Have students select three of the adjectives and create a 15–word sentence using their selected adjectives.

10. Instruct students to rewrite their 15 word sentences using one of the following templates:

Template 4

_____

_____   _____

_____   _____   _____

_____   _____   _____   _____

_____   _____   _____   _____   _____

Template 5

_____

_____   _____   _____   _____

_____   _____   _____   _____

_____   _____   _____

_____   _____

_____

Line Breaks and White Space *(cont.)*

11. Again, ask students to note which pattern created the best poem for their sentence.

12. Introduce the concept of white space by reading the following sentences and then showing the same sentences as they were turned into poems.

The frog jumped from log to log.

The

frog

     j   m   e
      u   p   d

from

    log

      to

        log.

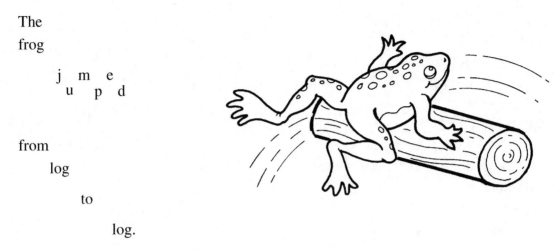

My ring was lost forever down the drain.

My ring

was

lost forever

d

   o

     w

       n

the drain.

13. Ask students if they notice anything unusual about the way the author wrote the words in these poems. Elicit ideas to explain why the author chose to create the lines that way.

14. Explain that authors sometimes use creativity in their poem layouts by using spacing and white space to create an effect.

15. Review the Line Breaks and White Space work sheet with students.

Line Breaks and White Space

1. Read the following poem.

    Weeping Willow
    Lonesome
    Trees
    Sit in the pale morning light,
    Guarding the shores of a
    Peaceful pond.
    A hazy mist hangs
    Over the trees and the dew-covered grass
        Like a veil.
    Faintly,
          In the distance,
    The howl of a dog and the mellow
    Trickling
    Of a stream
    Echoes   echoes
    Through the
    Empty
    Valley.

    I sit in the midst
    Of the saddened trees
    Wondering why
    They mourn.

2. What is the author's purpose in writing the poem?

    _____

    _____

3. Examine the poem line by line, word by word. What specific words or techniques has the author employed? How do they add to the overall effect of the poem?

    _____

    _____

    _____

    _____

Biography Poems
Teacher's Guide

Definition: A *biography poem* is written with biographical information about a specific person or several people in a specific group.

Materials Needed: Student Assignment Sheet (page 54), Family Interviews work sheet (page 55), Sample Biography Poem (page 56), Understanding a Biography Poem (page 57)

Preparation: Reproduce one copy of each work sheet for each student.

Lesson Plan: Review the Student Assignment Sheet with students. Tell students about the rubric that you will be using to assess their poetry (shown below). Give students a deadline for turning in their assignment.

Poetry Assessment Rubric

Criteria for **excellent** biography poems:

_____ The poem clearly focuses on the topic as a whole and each person within a given stanza.

_____ The poem uses precise words to create a vivid impression of the people being described.

_____ The poem has a rhythm that is obvious when the poem is read aloud.

_____ The author has strategically used white space and line breaks to create an intended effect.

_____ Spelling and punctuation are correct.

Criteria for **satisfactory** biography poems:

_____ The poem focuses on the topic as a whole and each person with a given stanza.

_____ The poem uses effective words to create an impression of the people being described.

_____ Most parts of the poem have definite rhythm when the poem is read aloud.

_____ The author has considered white space and line breaks in drafting the poem.

_____ Spelling and punctuation do not interfere with the meaning of the poem.

Criteria for **unsatisfactory** biography poems:

_____ The poem does not focus on the topic or the individuals within the stanzas.

_____ The author has not used effective words to create an impression of the people being described.

_____ The poem does not have a definite rhythm when read aloud.

_____ The author has not considered white space and line breaks in drafting the poem.

_____ Spelling and punctuation may interfere with the meaning of the poem.

Biography Poems
Student Assignment Sheet

A *biography poem* is written with biographical information about a specific person or several people in a specific group.

Getting Ready to Write

1. With a partner, list as many words as you can that begin with the prefix *bio-*.

2. Review with your partner what the prefix *bio-* means. Review with your partner what biography is.

3. Obtain the Family Interviews work sheet (page 55). List the members of your immediate family in the left hand column. Write their first names and their relationships to you.

4. In the next column, write four words that you would use to describe that person.

5. Take the interview sheet home. Interview each member of your family to complete the rest of the columns. Record their answers on the interview sheet. If you have a younger family member who could not answer the questions, it is all right to ask an adult to predict the child's answers.

6. Read the Sample Biography Poem (page 56) and complete the Understanding a Biography Poem work sheet (page 57). Note the structure and effectiveness of the poem.

Drafting

Use the information you gathered on your Family Interviews work sheet to begin drafting your biography poem by writing your family's last name as the first and last lines of the poem. Each stanza should be about a different family member.

Revising

When you have completed your draft, review your poem to make sure you have done the following:

- included all of the information from your interviews
- written separate stanzas about each person.
- punctuated your poem correctly to allow the reader to read it clearly
- used precise words to convey your purpose
- checked spelling

Applying Technology

Practice using the scanner to include pictures of your subjects. Once you have drafted the poem, scan pictures of your family members (or whoever your subjects are) into your word processing document. You can edit the size and placement of the pictures to best accompany your poem.

Family Interviews

Family member's name	Four words that describe this person	Three things this person loves	Two things this person needs	One thing this person fears	One thing this person wishes
	1. _____ 2. _____ 3. _____ 4. _____	1. _____ 2. _____ 3. _____	1. _____ 2. _____	1. _____	1. _____
	1. _____ 2. _____ 3. _____ 4. _____	1. _____ 2. _____ 3. _____	1. _____ 2. _____	1. _____	1. _____
	1. _____ 2. _____ 3. _____ 4. _____	1. _____ 2. _____ 3. _____	1. _____ 2. _____	1. _____	1. _____
	1. _____ 2. _____ 3. _____ 4. _____	1. _____ 2. _____ 3. _____	1. _____ 2. _____	1. _____	1. _____
	1. _____ 2. _____ 3. _____ 4. _____	1. _____ 2. _____ 3. _____	1. _____ 2. _____	1. _____	1. _____

Sample Biography Poem

Reiser

Frank
Tall, strong, hard-working,
    funny
Lover of animals, steak, and the
    Remote control
Who needs to work less
Who fears running out of gas in
    The harbor tunnel
Who wishes the grass would grow
    Slower in the summer.

Rachel
Petite, charming, warm, smart
Lover of sewing, books, and her
    Family
Who needs more hours in the day
Who fears growing old
Who wishes she was a gourmet
    Cook.

Brian
Big, loud, silly, happy
Lover of basketball, video
    Games, and bike riding
Who needs to have a bigger
    Allowance
Who fears having lots of
    Homework
Who wishes kids didn't have to
    Go to school.

Molly
Energetic, young, cute, cuddly
Lover of her teddy bear,
    Popsicles, and Sesame
    Street
Who needs to take a nap when she
    Gets cranky
Who fears scary noises in the
    Middle of the night
Who wishes she could stay up and
    Play all night long.

Reiser

Commentary

Try to guess the ages or relationships of each family member from the information you are given.

Understanding a Biography Poem

"Reiser"

1. How many stanzas are in this poem? _____

2. Why do you think the author chose this many stanzas? _____
_____

3. What do you notice about the first and last lines of the poem?_____
_____

4. How is this biography poem structured? _____
_____

5. What strikes you as particularly interesting about this poem?_____
_____

6. What writing techniques did the author employ? _____
_____

7. What was the author's purpose in choosing these techniques? _____
_____

8. Think of the purpose of a biography poem. Is this biography poem effective?_____
_____

9. What would you have done differently if you had written this poem? _____
_____

Idea Bank

1. Using information gathered from several resources write a biography poem about a historical figure who interests you.

2. Write a biography poem about a person for whom you know only a little bit. Such as a neighbor or faraway relative. Write it in a way that creates an impression or image of the person whom you are describing.

3. Use the lines below to capture your own ideas for biography poems.

_____

_____

_____

_____

_____

_____

_____

A Change Poem
Teacher's Guide

Definition: A *change poem* chronicles the change process of a being or concept. It is usually one sentence written with one word on each line. The poem has a surprising change at the end to complete the form.

Materials Needed: Student Assignment Sheet (page 59), Presto, Change-o! Cards (page 60), Sample Change Poems (pages 61–62), Understanding Change Poems (page 63)

Preparation: Reproduce one copy of the Student Assignment Sheet, Sample Change Poems, and Understanding Change Poems for each student. Reproduce one copy of the Presto, Change-o! Cards on card stock for each student. Cut the cards apart and put one set in each envelope for easy distribution.

Lesson Plan: Review the Student Assignment Sheet with students. Tell students about the rubric that you will be using to assess their poetry (shown below). Give students a deadline for turning in their assignment.

Poetry Assessment Rubric

Criteria for **excellent** change poems:

_____ The topic portrays a surprising change.

_____ The author has strategically placed words on lines to create an intended effect.

_____ The author uses precise word choices to portray a surprising change.

_____ Spelling and punctuation are correct.

Criteria for **satisfactory** change poems:

_____ The topic portrays a change.

_____ The author has placed one word on each line.

_____ The author uses effective word choices to portray a change.

_____ Spelling and punctuation do not interfere with the meaning of the poem.

Criteria for **unsatisfactory** change poems:

_____ The topic does not portray a significant change.

_____ The lines are not planned to reflect the change poem structure.

_____ The author does not use effective word choices to portray the change.

_____ Spelling and punctuation may interfere with the meaning of the poem.

A Change Poem
Student Assignment Sheet

A *change poem* chronicles the change process of a being or concept. It is usually one sentence written with one word on each line. The poem has a surprising change at the end to complete the form.

Getting Ready to Write

1. Using the Presto, Change-o! cards created by your teacher, read the word(s) on the front side of each card. On the back of each card, think of something into which the word could change. For example, if the front of the card says "day," you could write "night" on the back, because daytime changes into nighttime. Complete this activity for each card you have. For some words, you may have to stretch your imagination and be creative!

2. Pick a topic on one of your cards, or generate one of your own. If you decide to generate your own topic remember that you need two words that portray a changing relationship, such as day and night. Some of the most interesting change poems use topics that surprise the reader with the change.

3. Read the Sample Change Poems (pages 61–62) and complete the Understanding Change Poems work sheet (page 63). Note the structure and effectiveness of the poems.

Drafting

Write a sentence that shows the change in your chosen being or concept. Then, turn your sentence into a poem by rewriting your sentence, placing only one word on each line.

Revising

When you have completed your draft, review your poem to make sure you have . . .

- shown a change from one stage to another.
- written only one word on each line.
- used precise word choices to convey your purpose.

Applying Technology

Practice using the mouse and making hard returns. Using your original sentence, use the mouse to place the cursor in front of a word. Hit the return key to move this word to the next line. Continue in this manner until all of the words are on separate lines.

You could also practice using the cut and paste features of your computer. Again, using your original sentence, drag the mouse to highlight one word. Select the cut function from your tool bar. Use the mouse to place the cursor where you want the word placed. Select the paste function from your tool bar to insert the word where you want it. When you have finished rearranging your draft, print a copy of your poem.

Presto, Change-o! Cards

Directions to the teacher: Duplicate this page on card stock. You will need one copy for each student. Cut apart the cards and place in small envelopes for distribution to students during the lesson on page 58.

a little league baseball player	**baby**	**summer**
morning	**tadpole**	**puppy**
someone sleeping	**a car speeding on the highway**	**caterpillar**

Sample Change Poems

Winter	Commentary
winter	
snow	
melts	
and	
ice	
starts	
cracking	*Here is the beginning of the transition*
in	*to summer.*
a	
cool	
cup	
of	
lemonade	
on	
a	
hot	
summer	
day.	

Dairy	
The	
farmer	
squeezed	
the	
milk	
out	*This is a quicker transition—the milk goes right*
of	*from the cow to the cup.*
the	
cow	
into	
my	
cup.	

Sample Change Poems *(cont.)*

Growing Up	Commentary
The	
baby	
crawls	
across	
the	
floor	
and	
climbs	*Here is the transition.*
into	
the	
rocking	
chair	
while	
her	
grandchildren	
sit	
on	
her	
lap.	*What did the baby change into?*

The King	
Elvis	
young	
alive	
singing	
with	
joy	
through	
the	
power	
of	
his	
soul	
in	
heaven.	*The change occurs right at the end.*

Understanding Change Poems

"Winter"

1. What change is the author chronicling?_____

2. Why do you think the author chose this particular title for the poem?_____

3. What strikes you as particularly interesting about this poem?_____

4. How do you think the author got the idea for this topic? _____

5. What would you have done differently if you had written this poem? _____

"Dairy"

1. What change is the author chronicling?_____

2. Why do you think the author chose this particular title for the poem?_____

3. What strikes you as particularly interesting about this poem?_____

4. How do you think the author got the idea for this topic? _____

5. What would you have done differently if you had written this poem? _____

"Growing Up"

1. What change is the author chronicling?_____

2. Why do you think the author chose this particular title for the poem?_____

3. What strikes you as particularly interesting about this poem?_____

4. How do you think the author got the idea for this topic? _____

5. What would you have done differently if you had written this poem? _____

"The King"

1. What change is the author chronicling?_____

2. Why do you think the author chose this particular title for the poem?_____

3. What strikes you as particularly interesting about this poem?_____

4. How do you think the author got the idea for this topic? _____

5. What would you have done differently if you had written this poem? _____

Idea Bank

1. For a week or so, note any events or objects that change from one thing to another in your journal or on paper. Use these collected ideas for change poems.

2. Use the lines below to capture any additional ideas for generating change poems.

_____

_____

_____

_____

Character Poems
Teacher's Guide

Definition: A *character poem* is written with a persona other than that of the author. The speaker could be another person, a fictional character, a machine, an object, an animal, anything your imagination chooses.

Materials Needed: Student Assignment Sheet (page 65), Sample Character Poems (page 66–67), Understanding Character Poems (page 68–69)

Preparation: Reproduce one copy of each work sheet for each student.

Lesson Plan: Review the Student Assignment Sheet with students. Tell students about the rubric that you will be using to assess their poetry (shown below). Give students a deadline for turning in their assignment.

Poetry Assessment Rubric

Criteria for **excellent** character poems:

_____ The poem clearly expresses the voice of the character.

_____ The poem reflects a definite mood.

_____ The author has strategically used white space and line breaks to create an intended effect.

_____ The author uses precise word choices to enhance the effect of the poem

_____ The author uses writing techniques to enhance the effect of the poem.

_____ Spelling and punctuation are correct.

Criteria for **satisfactory** character poems:

_____ The poem expresses the voice of the character.

_____ The poem reflects a mood.

_____ The author has considered white space and line breaks in drafting the poem.

_____ The author uses effective word choices to enhance the effect of the poem.

_____ The author uses writing techniques to enhance the effect of the poem.

_____ Spelling and punctuation do not interfere with the meaning of the poem.

Criteria for **unsatisfactory** character poems:

_____ The poem does not express the voice of the character.

_____ The poem does not reflect a clear mood.

_____ The author has not considered white space and line breaks in drafting the poem.

_____ The author did not use effective word choices that enhance the effect of the poem.

_____ The author does not use writing techniques to enhance the effect of the poem.

_____ Spelling and punctuation may interfere with the meaning of the poem.

Character Poems
Student Assignment Sheet

A *character poem* is written with a persona other than that of the author. The speaker could be another person, a fictional character, a machine, an object, an animal, anything your imagination chooses.

Getting Ready to Write

1. Read the list of "characters" below as you think about writing a character poem using a persona other than your own. (*Note:* If your teacher has a prop box, you could select an item from the box instead of the list.)

   - a refrigerator
   - a curling iron
   - a zoo keeper
   - a sick person
   - a puppy

   - chewing gum
   - a math book
   - a dinosaur
   - a mountain
   - a tennis shoe

2. Pick one of the "characters" as the topic of your poem. Imagine that the item can talk, and write five statements that the item might say if it became a character.

3. Read the Sample Character Poems (pages 66–67). Complete the Understanding Character Poems work sheet (page 68–69). Note the structure and effectiveness of the poems.

Drafting

Expand your ideas of what your character might say. Write your character's words in poem form. You could choose to rhyme your poem or not, depending on the mood you wish to convey.

Revising

When you have completed your draft, review your poem to make sure you have . . .
- captured the voice of your character.
- used line breaks, white space, and writing techniques to enhance the effect of your poem.
- created the mood you wish to portray.
- used precise word choices to convey your purpose.

Applying Technology

Practice using watermarks to illustrate your work. After you have typed your draft in a word processing program, select the function that allows you to create watermarks as a background for your text. Choose an appropriate watermark for your poem. Once you have selected one that enhances the effect of your poem, print a copy.

Sample Character Poems

The Homeless

You see us when you walk on the
Street.
Sitting on the ground or lying
At your feet.
You turn your head with your
Nose in the air.
To let us know that you don't
Care.

You look at us as if it were a
Crime.
When we say "Hey, Buddy can you
Spare a dime?"
But you can say "no" and just
Turn away,
Without even as much as a look
Of dismay.

It's horrible the way we live
Each day.
When we have to eat what you
Throw away.
You live in a house,
We live on the street.
In a cardboard box, do you think
It has heat?

For we are not animals, we don't
Live in a zoo.
Can't you look in our eyes and
See we are human beings, too?
You have love, a family, a home.
We have nothing but emptiness;
We're alone.

So the next time you're walking
Down the street.
Please give some thought to the
Homeless you meet.
Can you send some love and
Kindness our way?
To brighten perhaps just one day.
For we are people, we had hopes
And dreams, too.
But we weren't born as lucky as
You.

Commentary

*The speaker in the poem is speaking to someone.
Who is "you"?*

Note the rhyme scheme—AABB.

A powerful line

What is the author's tone?

Couplet at the end

Thought-provoking, powerful ending

Sample Character Poems *(cont.)*

Grass

I am a blade of grass.
I am trampled on and rained on.
But worst of all, cats and dogs
Chew on me.
And once in a while, I get cut
Down.
But I grow back every time.
People stomp on me, birds feed on
Me,
And my friends across the way
Were dug up for a tree.
So go ahead, gimme your best
Shot.
'Cause I'll grow back!

Kenmore

Spaghetti sauce, I fear you not
Nor the chewing gum
Peanut butter, jelly too
Just adds to the fun!

Roll around and play some more
The grass is oh so green
Some puddles of mud, some
dried-up blood
It's not the worst I've seen.

In my mouth I'll take your clothes
And make them sparkling clean
For I'm the one, the only one
Your trusted washing machine!

Commentary

This author chose to tell the reader the persona in the first line. Does it help the reader understand the poem better or does it detract from the effect of the poem?

This is an internal rhyme—mud/blood.

Understanding Character Poems

"The Homeless"

1. Who is the speaker of the poem? _____

2. How do you know this? _____

3. Why do you think the author chose this particular title for the poem?_____

4. What strikes you as particularly interesting about this poem?_____

5. Which words paint the most vivid picture in your mind or create the strongest feelings? _____

6. What writing techniques did the author employ? _____

7. What was the author's purpose in choosing these techniques? _____

8. What is the tone of the poem?_____

9. Is this character poem effective? _____

10. What would you have done differently if you had written this poem? _____

"Grass"

1. Who is the speaker of the poem? _____

2. How do you know this? _____

3. Why do you think the author chose this particular title for the poem?_____

4. What strikes you as particularly interesting about this poem?_____

5. Which words paint the most vivid picture in your mind or create the strongest feelings? _____

6. What writing techniques did the author employ? _____

7. What was the author's purpose in choosing these techniques? _____

8. What is the tone of the poem?_____

9. Is this character poem effective? _____

10. What would you have done differently if you had written this poem? _____

Understanding Character Poems *(cont.)*

"Kenmore"

1. Who is the speaker of the poem? _____

   _____

2. How do you know this? _____

   _____

3. Why do you think the author chose this particular title for the poem?_____

   _____

4. What strikes you as particularly interesting about this poem?_____

   _____

5. Which words paint the most vivid picture in your mind or create the strongest feelings?

   _____

6. What writing techniques did the author employ? _____

   _____

7. What was the author's purpose in choosing these techniques? _____

   _____

8. What is the tone of the poem?_____

9. Is this character poem effective? _____

10. What would you have done differently if you had written this poem? _____

    _____

Idea Bank

1. Think of an inanimate object in a particular setting. For example, think of a snow plow sitting in an equipment lot on a sunny day, or of a spatula that is used in a restaurant that serves a lot of pancakes. Write a poem about the object's thoughts.

2. Think of two objects for which it might be fun to create a dialogue, such as the stapler and staple remover on a worker's desk or a tub of ice cream and a scoop. Write a poem that uses this dialogue.

3. Use the lines below to capture your own ideas for character poems.

   _____

   _____

   _____

   _____

   _____

   _____

   _____

Commentary Poems
Teacher's Guide

Definition: A *commentary poem* expresses your views on a subject. Most often, commentary poems express the poet's point of view on a controversial issue. You could write a commentary poem about a global issue such as homelessness or hunger, or you could write a commentary poem about a personal issue such as your bedtime or your household responsibilities.

Materials Needed: Student Assignment Sheet (page 71), Sample Commentary Poems (pages 72–73), Understanding Commentary Poems (page 74)

Preparation: Reproduce one copy of each work sheet for each student.

Lesson Plan: Review the Student Assignment Sheet with students. Tell students about the rubric that you will be using for assessment their poetry (shown below). Give students a deadline for turning in their assignment.

Poetry Assessment Rubric

Criteria for **excellent** commentary poems:

_____ The poem clearly expresses the poet's point of view.
_____ The poem evokes a strong feeling or mood.
_____ The author has strategically used white space and line breaks to create an intended effect.
_____ The author uses precise word choices to enhance the effect of the poem.
_____ The rhythm of the poem enhances the tone of the poem.
_____ The author uses writing techniques to enhance the effect of the poem.
_____ Spelling and punctuation are correct.

Criteria for **satisfactory** commentary poems:

_____ The poem expresses the poet's point of view.
_____ The poem evokes a feeling or mood.
_____ The author has considered white space and line breaks in drafting the poem.
_____ The author uses effective word choices to enhance the effect of the poem.
_____ The poem has an appropriate rhythm to match the tone of the poem.
_____ The author uses writing techniques to enhance the effect of the poem.
_____ Spelling and punctuation do not interfere with the meaning of the poem.

Criteria for **unsatisfactory** commentary poems:

_____ The poem does not express the poet's point of view.
_____ The poem does not evoke a feeling or mood.
_____ The author has not considered white space and line breaks in drafting the poem.
_____ The author uses poor word choices that do not enhance the effect of the poem.
_____ The rhythm is inappropriate for the tone of the poem.
_____ The author does not use writing techniques to enhance the effect of the poem.
_____ Spelling and punctuation may interfere with the meaning of the poem.

Commentary Poems
Student Assignment Sheet

A *commentary poem* expresses your views on a subject. Most often, commentary poems express the poet's point of view on a controversial issue. You could write a commentary poem about a global issue such as homelessness or hunger, or you could write a commentary poem about a personal issue such as your bedtime or your household responsibilities.

Getting Ready to Write

1. Think of issues that make you angry, that upset you, that you think are unfair. Jot them down in a brainstormed list.

2. Select one of the issues. Make sure it is one about which you feel strongly so that your poem will reflect your intense feelings.

3. Read the Sample Commentary Poems (pages 72–73) and complete the Understanding Commentary Poems work sheet (page 74). Note the structure and effectiveness of the poems.

Drafting

The best way to draft a commentary poem is simply to write your thoughts and feelings about a topic. Let all your feelings out and capture them on paper. Once you have your feelings out, then go back and reread what you have written. Use your knowledge of line breaks and white space to turn your drafting into poem form. Incorporate words and techniques that will enhance the tone of the poem.

Revising

When you have completed your draft, review your poem to make sure you have . . .

- clearly expressed your point of view.
- used line breaks, white space, and writing techniques to enhance the effect of your poem.
- created the mood you desire.
- created an appropriate rhythm for the tone of the poem.
- used precise word choices to convey your purpose.

Applying Technology

Practice using e-mail and sending attachments. Think of a person who would be interested in hearing your views on the topic you have chosen. It may be a friend, a relative, or a political figure such as a congress person or the President. Obtain the e-mail address for this person. E-mail a brief letter to the person, explaining your poem. Include a copy of your poem as an attachment to this letter.

Sample Commentary Poems

Away	Commentary
Walking past them on the street	
Seeing them on benches	*Who is the poet writing about?*
Their wrinkled faces	
Cringing in pain.	*What is the poet's tone?*
Lonely men and women	
In their "Golden Years"	
Quietly snoring,	
Not knowing where they are.	
Their children lock them away	
To get them out of their hair	
They visit them on holidays	
And maybe a couple of other	
times during the year	
If they feel like it.	
The government gives them money	
Enough to get by	
But is this enough	
for the men and women	*Notice how the poet uses "Golden Years" again—this time with a very different feeling.*
Whose "Golden Years"	
Are rusting?	*Unique, powerful ending*

Sample Commentary Poems *(cont.)*

This Is the House

This is the house that poverty built

Roaches and drugs and guns

This is the house that poverty built

Crime and dirtiness, hon

This is the house that poverty built

Killing and abandoned crack houses

This is the house that poverty built

Rats and spiders and mouses

This is the house that poverty built

People scared to walk around at night

This is the house that poverty built

Where even babies feel the fright

This is the house that poverty built

Hinges falling off the doors

This is the house that poverty built

Where we wish this could be ignored

This is the house that poverty built

Inhumane conditions for people to live

Politicians and citizens ridden with guilt

Because this is the house that poverty built.

Commentary

This poem not only rhymes, but twists a familiar line from a nursery rhyme. ("This is house that Jack built.") How do these techniques add to the poem's effect and tone?

Understanding Commentary Poems

"Away"

1. What is the author expressing? _____
2. What kind of person do you think the author is? _____
3. Why do you think the author chose this particular title for the poem?_____
   _____
4. What strikes you as particularly interesting about this poem?_____
   _____
5. Which words paint the most vivid pictures in your mind or evoke the strongest feelings?
   _____
6. What writing techniques did the author employ? _____
7. What was the author's purpose in choosing these techniques? _____
8. What is the tone of the poem?_____
9. Is the commentary poem effective? _____
10. What would you have done differently if you had written this poem? _____

"This Is the House"

1. What is the author expressing? _____
2. What kind of person do you think the author is? _____
3. Why do you think the author chose this particular title for the poem?_____
   _____
4. What strikes you as particularly interesting about this poem?_____
5. Which words paint the most vivid pictures in your mind or evoke the strongest feelings?
   _____
6. What writing techniques did the author employ? _____
7. What was the author's purpose in choosing these techniques? _____
8. What is the tone of the poem?_____
9. Is the commentary poem effective? _____
10. What would you have done differently if you had written this poem? _____

Idea Bank

1. Pay attention to your emotional responses as you listen to or watch the news. Use anything that evokes a strong response as a commentary poem.

2. Use the lines below to capture your ideas for commentary poems.

   _____

   _____

Curiosity Poems
Teacher's Guide

Definition: A *curiosity poem* poses questions about a part of life. The topic could be something the author dreams of, fears, or simply wonders about. Its purpose is to pose thoughtful questions and express the author's feelings toward the subject.

Materials Needed: Student Assignment Sheet (page 76), Sample Curiosity Poems (pages 77–78), Understanding Curiosity Poems (pages 79–80)

Preparation: Reproduce one copy of each work sheet for each student.

Lesson Plan: Review the Student Assignment Sheet with students. Tell students about the rubric that you will be using to assess their poetry (shown below). Give students a deadline for turning in their assignment.

Poetry Assessment Rubric

Criteria for **excellent** curiosity poems:

_____ The poem clearly focuses on the topic.

_____ The poem evokes a strong feeling or mood.

_____ The author has strategically used white space and line breaks to create an intended effect.

_____ The author uses precise word choices to enhance the effect of the poem.

_____ The author uses writing techniques to enhance the effect of the poem.

_____ Spelling and punctuation are correct.

Criteria for **satisfactory** curiosity poems:

_____ The poem focuses on the topic.

_____ The poem evokes a feeling or mood.

_____ The author has considered white space and line breaks in drafting the poem.

_____ The author uses effective word choices to enhance the effect of the poem.

_____ The author uses writing techniques to enhance the effect of the poem.

_____ Spelling and punctuation do not interfere with the meaning of the poem.

Criteria for **unsatisfactory** curiosity poems:

_____ The poem does not focus on the topic.

_____ The poem does not evoke a feeling or mood.

_____ The author has not considered white space and line breaks in drafting the poem.

_____ The author does not use effective word choices to enhance the effect of the poem.

_____ The author does not use writing techniques to enhance the effect of the poem.

_____ Spelling and punctuation may interfere with the meaning of the poem.

Curiosity Poems
Student Assignment Sheet

A *curiosity poem* poses questions about a part of life. The topic could be something the author dreams of, fears, or simply wonders about. Its purpose is to pose thoughtful questions and express the author's feelings toward the subject.

Getting Ready to Write

1. Sit with a partner and jot down a list of questions you have about the future. They could be questions related to your personal life such as, "What kind of job will I have?", or questions related to everyone's life, such as, "What is it like to die?"

2. Pick one of your questions to use as a poem topic. Write several more questions that relate to your chosen topic. For example, if you selected "What kind of job will I have?", you could add questions such as, "Will I make a lot of money?", "Will I have a college degree?", "Will I have to work long hours?".

3. Read the Sample Curiosity Poems (page 77–78) and complete the Understanding Curiosity Poems work sheets (page 79–80). Note the structure and effectiveness of the poems.

Drafting

Organize your topic questions. You may choose to reword or sequence them so that they rhyme. You may choose to use repetition and start several of the lines in the same manner. When you get to the end of your questions, create another question that sums up all of the other questions. (For a clear idea of how to do this, reread the samples.)

Revising

When you have completed your draft, review your poem to make sure you have . . .

- only used questions that pertain to your topic.
- written the questions in a logical order.
- summed up your poem with an ending question.
- used precise word choices to convey your tone and purpose.

Applying Technology

After you finish typing your draft, select a graphics or drawing program on your computer. Select or create a graphic of a large question mark. Create a border around your poem that is comprised of the question mark graphic. Print a copy of your poem with the border.

Sample Curiosity Poems

Getting Old

What happens when you get old?
Do you automatically start to
    wrinkle and fold?
Do you lose and gain new friends?
Do you start to wear new
    fashion trends?
Do you start liking
    orchestra and band?
Do people start calling you
    an old man?
Do you change your
    childhood tastes?
And at the thought of your age,
    do you become disgraced?
When you lose your hair,
    do you get mad?
Is getting old good or bad?

Commentary

Fold is an interesting word choice.
What does the poet mean by "lose and gain new friends"? Could there be a hidden meaning?

Here's the summary question.
What is the author's tone?

The Starter

What happens when you make it
    to the show?
Do people want your autograph
    wherever you go?
Does your arm get tired from
    pitching, then signing?
Do they ask your opinion about
    the new uniforms they're designing?
Do you always get free clothes
    from sports apparel companies?
Does your accountant oversee all
    your money and stocks?
Does your body hurt when you've
    played your last game?
Is arthritis a good price for fame?

Where does the title come from?

What is the author writing about?

Are any of the rhymes a little too forced?

Could the rhyme be changed to improve lines 5–9?

What is the author's tone at the end of the poem?

Sample Curiosity Poems *(cont.)*

Let's Take a Ride

What happens when you start to drive?
Do you always have to give your
    little brother a ride?
Do you worry about
    your car getting stolen?
Do you always have to tell
    your parents where you're
    goin'?
What happens when you take the
    wrong route?
Should I stare out my rear view
    mirror at the boy behind me
    who's awfully cute?
What should I do when I can't
    get out of the parking lot?
Or what happens when my
    air conditioning is broken
    and I'm really hot?
What happens when my tank shows
    I'm almost out of gas?
Should I start driving?
    I think I'll pass.

December 31

Is it easy to say goodbye?
Above the world, they're all so high.
I wonder if you learn to fly.
I wonder if you touch the sky.
I wonder what happens when you die.

Commentary

Who is the speaker in this poem?

This poem rhymes. How does this add to the tone of the poem?

Why did the author choose this title?

What is the author wondering about? How does the repetition of "I wonder" affect the poem?

Understanding Curiosity Poems

"Getting Old"

1. What is the author wondering about? _____

2. Why do you think the author chose this particular title for the poem?_____
   _____

3. What strikes you as particularly interesting about this poem?_____
   _____

4. What is the author's tone or feeling toward the subject? _____
   _____

5. What writing techniques did the author employ? _____
   _____

6. What was the author's purpose in choosing these techniques? _____
   _____

7. Is the curiosity poem effective? _____
   _____

8. What would you have done differently if you had written this poem? _____
   _____

"The Starter"

1. What is the author wondering about? _____
   _____

2. Why do you think the author chose this particular title for the poem?_____
   _____

3. What strikes you as particularly interesting about this poem?_____
   _____

4. What is the author's tone or feeling toward the subject? _____
   _____

5. What writing techniques did the author employ? _____
   _____

6. What was the author's purpose in choosing these techniques? _____
   _____

7. Is the curiosity poem effective? _____
   _____

8. What would you have done differently if you had written this poem? _____
   _____

Understanding Curiosity Poems *(cont.)*

"Let's Take a Ride"

1. What is the author wondering about? _____
2. Why do you think the author chose this particular title for the poem?_____
   _____
3. What strikes you as particularly interesting about this poem?_____
   _____
4. What is the author's tone or feeling toward the subject? _____
   _____
5. What writing techniques did the author employ? _____
6. What was the author's purpose in choosing these techniques? _____
   _____
7. Is the curiosity poem effective? _____
   _____
8. What would you have done differently if you had written this poem? _____
   _____

"December 31"

1. What is the author wondering about? _____
2. Why do you think the author chose this particular title for the poem?_____
   _____
3. What strikes you as particularly interesting about this poem?_____
   _____
4. What is the author's tone or feeling toward the subject? _____
   _____
5. What writing techniques did the author employ? _____
   _____
6. What was the author's purpose in choosing these techniques? _____
   _____
7. Is the curiosity poem effective? _____
8. What would you have done differently if you had written this poem? _____
   _____

Idea Bank

1. What were you curious about when you were younger? Did you have any amusing ideas that might be good material for a poem? Write it.
2. Think about a historical period that interests you. Write a curiosity poem about how it must have felt to live during that period.
3. Use the lines below to capture your ideas for curiosity poems.

   _____
   _____

Definition Poems
Teacher's Guide

Definition: A *definition poem* uses metaphorical language to define an abstract concept or a concrete object. The poet could create one comparison and expand the idea or present several different comparisons in the poem.

Materials Needed: Student Assignment Sheet (page 82), Definition Poem Topics (page 83), Sample Definition Poems (pages 84–85), Understanding Definition Poems (pages 86–87)

Preparation: Reproduce one copy of each work sheet for each student.

Lesson Plan: Review the Student Assignment Sheet with students. Tell students about the rubric that you will be using to assess their poems (shown below). Give students a deadline for turning in their assignment.

Poetry Assessment Rubric

Criteria for **excellent** definition poems:

_____ The poem clearly defines the topic.

_____ The poem evokes a strong feeling or mood.

_____ The author has strategically used white space and line breaks to create an intended effect.

_____ The author uses precise word choices to enhance the effect of the poem.

_____ The author uses writing techniques to enhance the effect of the poem.

_____ Spelling and punctuation are correct.

Criteria for **satisfactory** definition poems:

_____ The poem defines the topic.

_____ The poem evokes a feeling or mood.

_____ The author has considered white space and line breaks in drafting the poem.

_____ The author uses effective word choices to enhance the effect of the poem.

_____ The author uses writing techniques to enhance the effect of the poem.

_____ Spelling and punctuation do not interfere with the meaning of the poem.

Criteria for **unsatisfactory** definition poems:

_____ The poem does not define the topic.

_____ The poem does not evoke a feeling or mood.

_____ The author has not considered white space and line breaks in drafting the poem.

_____ The author did not use effective word choices to enhance the effect of the poem.

_____ The author does not use writing techniques to enhance the effect of the poem.

_____ Spelling and punctuation may interfere with the meaning of the poem.

Writing a Definition Poem
Student Assignment Sheet

A *definition poem* uses metaphorical language to define an abstract concept or concrete object. The poet could create one comparison and expand the idea or present several different comparisons in the poem.

Getting Ready to Write

1. Review the definition of a metaphor.

2. Choose a topic from the Definition Poem Topics work sheet (page 83) for your definition poem. You could choose to write about an abstraction such as life or love, or you could write metaphorically about a concrete object such as grass or sand.

3. Brainstorm comparisons between your topic and something else. You could either create one comparison and expand your thoughts or create several comparisons for your topic.

4. Read the Sample Definition Poems (pages 84–85) and complete the Understanding Definition Poems work sheets (pages 86–87). Note the structure and effectiveness of the poems.

Drafting

Draft your comparisons into poem form. You will need to decide whether you want your poem to rhyme or not, depending on the mood you wish to create. Be sure to use precise words to express your ideas clearly.

Revising

When you have completed your draft, review your poem to make sure you have . . .

- created a definition of your topic using metaphorical language.
- used line breaks, white space, and writing techniques to enhance the effect of your poem.
- created the tone you wish to portray.
- used precise word choices to convey your purpose.

Applying Technology

Practice using different size fonts for your poem. Once you have typed your draft into the computer, use the mouse to select your entire poem. Select a different size font for your definition poem from the tool bar. Once you are satisfied with the size you have chosen, print a copy of your poem.

Definition Poem Topics

Choose from one of the following topics for your definition poem.

Abstractions

- death
- love
- hatred
- life
- injustice
- anger
- sorrow
- sadness
- joy
- peace
- friendship
- generosity
- prejudice
- jealousy
- pride
- anxiety
- hope
- courage
- fear
- loneliness
- freedom
- peace
- war
- liberty
- happiness
- insecurity

Concrete Objects

- grass
- sand
- snow
- ice
- wind
- rain
- sunshine
- mountains
- clouds
- sky
- tears
- blood

Sample Definition Poems

The Maze	**Commentary**
Life is a maze of choices and decisions.	*Here is a metaphor.*
Each choice gives you different options.	*The rest of the poem expands on the one comparison.*
If you watch what you're doing, the maze will be easy to finish.	
If you aren't careful and you make a wrong turn,	
you could run into a dead end.	*Could the dead end be taken literally?*
Occasionally, you can change your course.	
But remember, you could only get one chance to live.	
Choose wisely.	*What is the author's tone?*

Jealousy

Jealousy is a disguise for hatred and anger and fear.	*This poem presents several comparisons.*
Jealousy is hiding behind a mask of hurt and sorrow and pain.	*How does the repetition affect the poem?*
Jealousy is a teasing game of "I can't have," a strong desire.	
Jealousy is a possessive force even for loved ones.	*What is the author's tone?*

Sample Definition Poems *(cont.)*

Loneliness

Loneliness is
>a distant train whistle
>>moaning and mournful.

Loneliness is one
>isolated
>>quietness.

Loneliness is hot tears
>that drown
>>the soul.

Loneliness is emptiness
>waiting to be filled.

Commentary

What is the author's tone?

Hot tears gives the poem a tactile sense.

The Pond of Life

Life is a frozen pond.
I'm skating on it.
I glide over the surface,
Testing the ice.
I speed up as I go,
Only to lose speed as I hit
bare areas.
Little kids appear and I must
try to dodge them,
Thud! A child runs into me.
I find myself on the ground, my
face in the snow,
Tangled in a heap.
I get up and skate on.
This time with fear.
The world is hard and cold.
I slip and fall again.
I skate on,
this time with vengeance.
The world is mine.
I know how to skate this pond.

This poem presents one comparison, extended throughout its lines.

What is the author's tone?

What do the bare areas represent? What do the little kids represent?

How is the author paralleling life?

What is the author's tone? Does his tone change during the poem?

Understanding Definition Poems

"The Maze"

1. What is the author comparing in the poem's metaphor? _____
_____

2. Why do you think the author chose this particular title for the poem?_____
_____

3. What strikes you as particularly interesting about this poem?_____
_____

4. Which words paint the most vivid picture in your mind or evoke the strongest feelings?
_____

5. What writing techniques did the author employ? _____
_____

6. What was the author's purpose in choosing these techniques? _____
_____

7. What is the tone of the poem?_____
_____

8. Is this definition poem effective? _____
_____

9. What would you have done differently if you had written this poem? _____
_____

"Jealousy"

1. Why do you think the author chose this particular title for the poem?_____
_____

2. What strikes you as particularly interesting about this poem?_____
_____

3. Which words paint the most vivid picture in your mind or evoke the strongest feelings?
_____

4. What writing techniques did the author employ? _____
_____

5. What was the author's purpose in choosing these techniques? _____
_____

6. What is the tone of the poem?_____
_____

7. Is this definition poem effective? _____
_____

8. What would you have done differently if you had written this poem? _____
_____

Understanding Definition Poems *(cont.)*

"Loneliness"

1. What is the author comparing in the metaphor? _____

_____

2. Why do you think the author chose this particular title for the poem?_____

_____

3. What strikes you as particularly interesting about this poem?_____

_____

4. Which words paint the most vivid picture in your mind or evoke the strongest feelings?

_____

5. What writing techniques did the author employ? _____

_____

6. What was the author's purpose in choosing these techniques? _____

_____

7. What is the tone of the poem? _____

_____

8. Is this definition poem effective? _____

_____

9. What would you have done differently if you had written this poem? _____

_____

"The Pond of Life"

1. What is the author comparing in the metaphor? _____

_____

2. Why do you think the author chose this particular title for the poem?_____

_____

3. What strikes you as particularly interesting about this poem?_____

_____

4. Which words paint the most vivid picture in your mind or evoke the strongest feelings?

_____

5. What writing techniques did the author employ? _____

_____

6. What was the author's purpose in choosing these techniques? _____

_____

7. What is the tone of the poem? _____

_____

8. Is this definition poem effective? _____

_____

9. What would you have done differently if you had written this poem? _____

_____

Event Poems
Teacher's Guide

Definition: An *event poem* uses highly descriptive language and writing techniques to portray an event or occurrence. The poem describes the sequence of steps in the event, while evoking strong sensory images and feelings.

Materials Needed: Student Assignment Sheet (page 89), Sample Event Poems (page 90–91), Understanding Event Poems (page 92–93)

Preparation: Reproduce one copy of each work sheet for each student.

Lesson Plan: Review the Student Assignment Sheet with students. Tell students about the rubric that you will be using to assess their poems (shown below). Give students a deadline for turning in their assignment.

Poetry Assessment Rubric

Criteria for **excellent** event poems:

_____ The poem clearly focuses on a narrow event.
_____ The poem evokes strong sensory images.
_____ The poem evokes a strong feeling or mood.
_____ The author has strategically used white space and line breaks to create an intended effect.
_____ The author uses precise word choices to vividly depict the event.
_____ The author uses writing techniques to enhance the effect of the poem.
_____ Spelling and punctuation are correct.

Criteria for **satisfactory** event poems:

_____ The poem focuses on a narrow topic.
_____ The poem evokes sensory images.
_____ The poem evokes a feeling or mood.
_____ The author has considered white space and line breaks in drafting the poem.
_____ The author uses effective word choices to depict the event.
_____ The author uses writing techniques to enhance the effect of the poem.
_____ Spelling and punctuation do not interfere with the meaning of the poem.

Criteria for **unsatisfactory** event poems:

_____ The poem does not focus on a narrow event.
_____ The poem does not evoke sensory images.
_____ The poem does not evoke a feeling or mood.
_____ The author has not considered white space and line breaks in drafting the poem.
_____ The author uses poor word choice that does not depict the event.
_____ The author does not use effective word choices to enhance the effect of the poem.
_____ The author does not use writing techniques to enhance the effect of the poem.
_____ Spelling and punctuation may interfere with the meaning of the poem.

Event Poems
Student Assignment Sheet

An *event poem* uses highly descriptive language and writing techniques to portray an event or occurrence. The poem describes the sequence of steps in the event, while evoking strong sensory images and feelings.

Getting Ready to Write

1. With a partner, brainstorm a list of occurrences or events. Your list could include traditional events such as a baseball game, a parade, or a birthday. Your list could also include smaller events like blowing a bubble, curling your hair, or brushing your teeth. Be creative and use your imagination.

2. Once you have exhausted your brain, choose one of the events to use as a topic for your poem. If you have selected a significant event such as a birthday, you will need to narrow your topic even further to "blowing out the candles on a cake" or "opening presents."

3. Have your topic approved by your teacher before continuing.

4. Read the Sample Event Poems (pages 90–91) and complete the Understanding Event Poems work sheets (pages 92–93). Note the structure and effectiveness of the poems.

Drafting

Think of what happens during your chosen event. Think of the correct sequence of steps. Draft your event poem, keeping your steps in proper sequence. Since your event is a very narrow topic, you will need to make your poem interesting by choosing descriptive words and incorporating various writing techniques.

Revising

When you have completed your draft, review your poem to make sure you have . . .

- written about a narrow topic.
- used line breaks, white space, and writing techniques to enhance the effect of your poem.
- created the tone you wish to portray.
- used precise word choices to convey your purpose.

Applying Technology

Practice using the thesaurus on your computer as you draft your poem. When you need a different word or want to incorporate a more specific word, select the thesaurus feature on your computer. Enter the word you wish to replace and scan the choices until you find a word you prefer. You may need to consult a dictionary to understand the different shades of meaning among words.

Sample Event Poems

Flames	**Commentary**
Crackling flames jump from log to log, trying to find the right one to whittle down into nothingness. Nibble. Nibble. Until natural wood turns into ashes, as black as they can be. Much warmth comes from the hearth. Jump! Jump! Crackle! Crackle! More flames join the frenzy. Soon there is only one lonely log, waiting to be burnt to a crisp. Poor little log. Will it ever survive the fire?	*Notice the personification throughout the poem.* *Frenzy is a great word to describe a roaring fire.* *Now the poet is focusing on only one log. Why?*

Losing the Battle

The hot spicy fire burns and
    burns.
The fire is king of the night.
    Boom! Crackle! Bang!
The wood crumbled into the hands
    of the almighty king.
The flames fly into the sky.
The firemen are losing the
    battle.
The building is crying for help.
But nothing can save it now.
The powerful king has conquered.
	Spicy—*interesting use of taste word*
	
	Notice the metaphor throughout the poem of the fire as a king in battle.
	
	Here is alliteration and internal rhyme ("flames fly into the sky").
	
	There is a good deal of personification in this poem.

Sample Event Poems *(cont.)*

Is the Old Man Still Snoring?

SPLASH!
pitter patter
Falling softly at first,
then more **heavily**
until infinite drops parachute
to the ground with a splish and a splatter and a
STRIKE!!
The sound of bowling pins
toppling
echoes through the gusty wind.
FLASH!
Electric beams flash down from
the heavens
to destroy anything
in their path.
SPLASH! STRIKE! FLASH!

Commentary

This poem makes use of onomatopoeia.

Why is the word heavily *bold?*
Here is a unique use of parachut

Notice the double meaning of strike.

All three sounds are repeated.

Coin-Operated

Traveling into a churning stomach
Chemical suds
boil on its sides
Brushes swipe furiously
at the metal germ
Pushing it along
Intense suction
dries it off
The germ,
now sterile,
speeds up,
comes out the other end
with a lively squeal.
"Hey, buddy.
You want us to
wax your car, too?"

Here is a metaphor.

What is the germ? What is the poet writing about?

Understanding Event Poems

"Flames"

1. What is the author describing? _____
   _____

2. Why do you think the author chose this particular title for the poem? _____
   _____

3. What strikes you as particularly interesting about this poem? _____
   _____

4. Which words paint the most vivid pictures in your mind? _____
   _____

5. What writing techniques did the author employ? _____
   _____

6. What was the author's purpose in choosing these techniques? _____
   _____

7. What feelings or emotions do you experience after reading this poem? _____
   _____

8. Is this event poem effective? _____
   _____

9. What would you have done differently if you had written this poem? _____
   _____

"Losing the Battle"

1. What is the author describing? _____
   _____

2. Why do you think the author chose this particular title for the poem? _____
   _____

3. What strikes you as particularly interesting about this poem? _____
   _____

4. Which words paint the most vivid picture in your mind? _____
   _____

5. What writing techniques did the author employ? _____
   _____

6. What was the author's purpose in choosing these techniques? _____
   _____

7. What feelings or emotions do you experience after reading this poem? _____
   _____

8. Is this event poem effective? _____
   _____

9. What would you have done differently if you had written this poem? _____
   _____

Understanding Event Poems *(cont.)*

"Is the Old Man Still Snoring?"

1. What is the author describing? _____
2. Why do you think the author chose this particular title for the poem?_____
   _____
3. What strikes you as particularly interesting about this poem?_____
   _____
4. Which words paint the most vivid picture in your mind? _____
   _____
5. What writing techniques did the author employ? _____
   _____
6. What was the author's purpose in choosing these techniques? _____
   _____
7. What feelings or emotions do you experience after reading this poem?_____
   _____
8. Is this event poem effective? _____
9. What would you have done differently if you had written this poem? _____
   _____

"Coin-Operated"

1. What is the author describing? _____
2. Why do you think the author chose this particular title for the poem?_____
   _____
3. What strikes you as particularly interesting about this poem?_____
   _____
4. Which words paint the most vivid picture in your mind? _____
   _____
5. What writing techniques did the author employ? _____
   _____
6. What was the author's purpose in choosing these techniques? _____
   _____
7. What feelings or emotions do you experience after reading this poem?_____
   _____
8. Is this event poem effective? _____
9. What would you have done differently if you had written this poem? _____
   _____

Idea Bank

1. Look in the newspaper for an odd event, such as one about someone who owns too many pets, and use it as the basis for a poem.
2. Write a poem about an event that you wish you could have attended, such as the presidential inauguration.

Found Poems
Teacher's Guide

Definition: A *found poem* is created from text or conversation. The original text or conversation was not intended to be a poem; the author of a found poem literally finds the words from a book, magazine, flyer, conversation, etc., and turns them into a poem.

Materials Needed: Student Assignment Sheet (page 95), Samples of Found Poems (page 96–97), Understanding Found Poems (page 98–99)

Preparation: Reproduce one copy of each work sheet for each student.

Lesson Plan: Review the Student Assignment Sheet with students. Tell students about the rubric that you will be using to assess their poems (shown below). Give students a deadline for turning in their assignment.

Poetry Assessment Rubric

Criteria for **excellent** found poems:

_____ The poem clearly focuses on a topic.

_____ The poem uses specifically chosen words to create an interesting topic.

_____ The author has strategically used white space and line breaks to create an intended effect.

_____ Spelling and punctuation are correct (if applicable).

Criteria for **satisfactory** found poems:

_____ The poem focuses on a topic.

_____ The poem uses selected words to create a topic.

_____ The author has considered white space and line breaks in drafting the poem.

_____ Spelling and punctuation do not interfere with the meaning of the poem (if applicable).

Criteria for **unsatisfactory** found poems:

_____ The poem does not focus on a topic.

_____ The author has not chosen appropriate words to create a topic.

_____ The author has not considered white space and line breaks in drafting the poem.

_____ Spelling and punctuation may interfere with the meaning of the poem (if applicable).

Found Poems
Student Assignment Sheet

A *found poem* is a poem that has been created from text or conversation. The original text or conversation was not intended to be a poem; the author of a found poem literally finds the words from a book, magazine, flyer, conversation, etc., and turns them into a poem.

Getting Ready to Write

1. Gather some words to use in your poem by selecting a location for some quality eavesdropping—in your home, the cafeteria, the shopping mall, the doctor's office, or anywhere you might overhear some conversation. Take a pad of paper and a pen or pencil to your chosen spot. Sit for at least ten minutes, listening to bits and pieces of any conversations that may be going on around you. While listening, do your best to jot down the bits of conversation you hear. It is not necessary for you to record all of a conversation or to hear all sides of the conversation—bits and pieces here and there actually create a more interesting poem!

   Alternatively, you may flip through a magazine or newspaper, cutting out interesting phrases and words, or skim a book that you are reading for interesting words and phrases. Jot them down.

2. Read the Sample Found Poems (pages 96–97) and complete the Understanding Found Poems work sheets (pages 99–100). Note the structure and effectiveness of the poems.

Drafting

Review the notes you took from your eavesdropping session or from your list of words and phrases from the newspaper, magazine, or book. Pick out words, phrases, or sentences that you think are especially poetic. Arrange the words as lines in a poem, paying particular attention to line breaks, white space, capitalization, and punctuation. When creating a found poem, you can leave out words from the original conversation or text, but you cannot add words or change the order of words.

Revising

When you have completed your draft, review your poem to make sure you have . . .

- written the words in the form of a poem.
- kept the words in the same order and did not add any words.
- arranged the words so that the poem has a purpose and makes sense.

Applying Technology

Practice highlighting and deleting words and phrases from your text. Type your notes into a word processing document. As you draft the notes into a poem, drag the mouse to highlight a word or phrase that you do not wish to include in your poem. After the text is highlighted, hit the delete key to erase this portion of text. You could also practice using the cut function to achieve the same result.

Sample Found Poems

5:15

"Hey, that's my glove!"

"What's for dinner, honey?"

"I'm going out."

"No snacking, dinner's almost ready."

"Mom! Phone!"

"Aarf! Aarf! Aarf!"

"Ok, 'bye."

"Have you seen my . . ."

    "DINNER!"

Camden Yards

"Batting third . . . Cal . . .Cal . . .

    Ripken . . . Ripken."

"Number eight, he's so great."

    (giggle)

    "Peanuts! Popcorn!"

" . . . million dollar contract . . ."

    "Cracker Jacks!"

"Strike two!"

    "Come on, come on."

" . . . man on third . . ."

"He can do it if anyone can."

    "Eew! I stepped on gum!"

"Home run!"

    "Yeah!"

Commentary

How many people are in this conversation?

Where did the title come from?

What is being overheard?

Why did the author use repetition here?

What happens in this poem?

Sample Found Poems *(cont.)*

Commentary

What is the author's opinion of chocolate chip cookies?

What is ironic about this ending?

Farm Fresh Milk

MISSING

Date: 5/12/78
From: New Jersey
White Female
3 Ft 2 in
5 Years Old

Commentary

The Face on the Milk Carton

Missing
Jane Elizabeth Johnson, kidnapping of
New Jersey
Kidnapped at age five . . .
Social Workers and Newspaper Reporters
And TV cameras and -
"Hello?"
"Hi."
"It's . . ."
"Your Daughter."
"Me!!"
"Jenny Spring."

What happens in this poem?

Understanding Found Poems

"5:15"

1. What is the author's source for the words in this poem? _____

    _____

2. What is the topic of the poem? _____

    _____

3. What is the author's tone or attitude toward the topic? What specific words give you this idea?

    _____

4. What strikes you as particularly interesting about this poem?_____

    _____

5. What writing techniques did the author employ? _____

    _____

6. What was the author's purpose in choosing these techniques? _____

    _____

7. Is the found poem effective? _____

    _____

8. What would you have done differently if you had written this poem? _____

    _____

"Camden Yards"

1. What is the author's source for the words in this poem? a book? a magazine? newspaper? conversation? other?

    _____

2. What is the topic of the poem? _____

    _____

3. What is the author's tone or attitude toward the topic? What specific words give you this idea?

    _____

4. What strikes you as particularly interesting about this poem?_____

    _____

5. What writing techniques did the author employ? _____

    _____

6. What was the author's purpose in choosing these techniques? _____

    _____

7. Is the found poem effective? _____

    _____

8. What would you have done differently if you had written this poem? _____

    _____

Understanding Found Poems *(cont.)*

"Homemade Chewy Chocolate Chip Cookies"

1. What is the author's source for the words in this poem? _____
   _____
2. What is the topic of the poem? _____
3. What is the author's tone or attitude toward the topic? What specific words give you this
   idea?_____
4. What strikes you as particularly interesting about this poem?_____
   _____
5. What writing techniques did the author employ? _____
   _____
6. What was the author's purpose in choosing these techniques? _____
   _____
7. Is this found poem effective? _____
8. What would you have done differently if you had written this poem? _____
   _____

"The Face on the Milk Carton"

1. What is the author's source for the words in this poem? a book? a magazine?
   newspaper? conversation? other? _____
   _____
2. What is the topic of the poem? _____
3. What is the author's tone or attitude toward the topic? What specific words give you this
   idea?_____
4. What strikes you as particularly interesting about this poem?_____
   _____
5. What writing techniques did the author employ? _____
   _____
6. What was the author's purpose in choosing these techniques? _____
   _____
7. Is this found poem effective? _____
8. What would you have done differently if you had written this poem? _____
   _____

Idea Bank

1. Open a book, close your eyes, flip through the book, and point at a word. Open your
   eyes and write the word down on a piece of paper. Repeat several times. Now try to
   use the words together in a poem.
2. Look for scraps of paper on the sidewalk or around the house. Write down the contents
   of the scraps as a found poem.

_____

_____

_____

Standards and Benchmarks: 1A, 1B, 1C, 1D, 3I

Future Poems
Teacher's Guide

Definition: A *future poem* asks the poet to look into the future and imagine how life will be. The poet may write about the life he or she imagines personally—future job, family life, finances, or the future of the world as a whole.

Materials Needed: Student Assignment Sheet (page 102), Now and Then graphic organizer (page 103), Sample of Future Poems (page 104), Understanding Future Poems (page 105)

Preparation: Reproduce one copy of each work sheet for each student.

Lesson Plan: Review the Student Assignment Sheet with students. Tell them about the rubric that you will be using to assess their poems (shown below). Give students a deadline for turning in their assignment.

Poetry Assessment Rubric

Criteria for **excellent** future poems:

_____ The poem clearly focuses on the topic.

_____ The poem evokes a strong feeling or mood.

_____ The author has strategically used white space and line breaks to create an intended effect.

_____ The author uses precise word choices to enhance the effect of the poem.

_____ The author uses writing techniques to enhance the effect of the poem.

_____ Spelling and punctuation are correct.

Criteria for **satisfactory** future poems:

_____ The poem focuses on the topic.

_____ The poem evokes a feeling or mood.

_____ The author has considered white space and line breaks in drafting the poem.

_____ The author uses effective word choices to enhance the effect of the poem.

_____ Spelling and punctuation do not interfere with the meaning of the poem.

Criteria for **unsatisfactory** future poems:

_____ The poem does not focus on the topic.

_____ The poem does not evoke a feeling or mood.

_____ The author has not considered white space and line breaks in drafting the poem.

_____ The author does not use effective word choices to enhance the effect of the poem.

_____ The author does not use writing techniques to enhance the effect of the poem.

_____ Spelling and punctuation may interfere with the meaning of the poem.

Writing a Future Poem
Student Assignment Sheet

> A *future poem* asks the poet to look into the future and imagine how life will be. The poet may write about the life they imagine personally—their future job, family life, finances—or the future of the world as a whole.

Getting Ready to Write

1. Imagine that it is the year 2020. Figure out how old you will be and jot it down.

2. Complete the Now and Then graphic organizer (page 103). For each category, describe how things are now and how you imagine they will be in the year 2020.

3. Share your ideas with a partner.

4. Read the Sample Future Poem (page 104) and complete the Understanding Future Poems work sheet (page 105). Note the structure and effectiveness of the poems.

Drafting

Use the ideas you generated on the Now and Then graphic organizer to draft a future poem. Remember, your future poem could be about the future of the world or your personal future. Try to focus the subject of your poem to one specific aspect of life.

Revising

When you have completed your draft, review your poem to make sure you have . . .

- focused your topic.
- used line breaks, white space, and writing techniques to enhance the effect of your poem.
- created the tone you wish to portray.
- used precise word choices to convey your purpose.

Applying Technology

Practice using different types of fonts with your future poem. After you have typed your draft in a word processing program, drag your mouse across the entire poem to highlight it or simply "select all." Then, using the font feature on your tool bar, select different fonts for your poem. Once you have selected one that enhances the effect of your poem, print a copy.

Now and Then

Directions: Complete the following chart. For each category, describe how things are now and how you imagine them being in the year 2020.

Category	Now (Year _____)	In the year 2020
Transportation		
Government		
Environment		
Finances		
Health		
Fashion		
Entertainment		
Communication		

Sample Future Poem

My Dream

I will lift my scalpel and
correct the eyes of those
who have never seen.
I will help them see
a beautiful world
and everything in between.

I will give the world the gift
of sight,
how wonderful that will be.
I will let them see the blue,
the yellow,
and even the teal and green.

Like a luminous sunset,
deepened with shadowy hues and
misty colors,
I will shine through the night,
and share beauty with others.

Commentary

This poem rhymes.

What is the poet writing about?

Notice the simile.
Great words to describe a sunset.

What is the author's tone?

Understanding Future Poems

"My Dream"

1. What aspect of the future is the author writing about? _____

   _____

2. Why do you think the author chose this particular title for the poem?_____

   _____

3. What strikes you as particularly interesting about this poem?_____

   _____

4. Which words paint the most vivid picture in your mind? _____

   _____

5. What writing techniques did the author employ? _____

   _____

6. What was the author's purpose in choosing these techniques? _____

   _____

7. What is the author's tone in this poem?_____

   _____

8. Is this future poem effective? _____

   _____

9. What would you have done differently if you had written this poem? _____

   _____

Idea Bank

1. Think of a future event to which you are not looking forward, such as a major test. Write your feelings about this future event.

2. As an innovation to a future poem, write a prediction poem about an event that will happen a few days from now. Put it aside. After the event, add to the poem by writing about what actually happened and your feelings and ideas about it.

3. Use the lines below to capture your own ideas for future poems.

   _____

   _____

   _____

   _____

   _____

   _____

   _____

Love Poems
Teacher's Guide

Definition: A *love poem* captures the essence of a loving relationship using words. A love poem could be written about any subject—as long as love is the central theme. Many love poems are written about people; however, a love poem could be written about inanimate objects or animals as well.

Materials Needed: Student Assignment Sheet (page 107), Sample Love Poems (page 108), Understanding Future Poems (page 109)

Preparation: Reproduce one copy of each work sheet for each student.

Lesson Plan: Review the Student Assignment Sheet with students. Tell them about the rubric that you will be using to assess their poems (shown below). Give students a deadline for turning in their assignment.

Poetry Assessment Rubric

Criteria for **excellent** love poems:

_____ The poem clearly captures the essence of the loving relationship.

_____ The author has strategically used white space and line breaks to create an intended effect.

_____ The author uses precise word choices to enhance the effect of the poem.

_____ The author uses writing techniques to enhance the effect of the poem.

_____ Spelling and punctuation are correct.

Criteria for **satisfactory** love poems:

_____ The poem captures the essence of the loving relationship.

_____ The author has considered white space and line breaks in drafting the poem.

_____ The author uses effective word choices to enhance the effect of the poem.

_____ The author uses writing techniques to enhance the effect of the poem.

_____ Spelling and punctuation do not interfere with the meaning of the poem.

Criteria for **unsatisfactory** love poems:

_____ The poem does not capture the essence of the loving relationship.

_____ The author has not considered white space and line breaks in drafting the poem.

_____ The author does not use effective word choices to enhance the effect of the poem.

_____ The author does not use writing techniques to enhance the effect of the poem.

_____ Spelling and punctuation may interfere with the meaning of the poem.

Love Poems
Student Assignment Sheet

> A *love poem* captures the essence of a loving relationship using words. A love poem could be written about any subject—as long as love is the central theme. Many love poems are written about people; however, a love poem could be written about inanimate objects or animals, as well.

Getting Ready to Write

1. Think of someone you love, or alternatively, think of a loving relationship that could occur between two objects or animals (for example, a pen and paper, a cat and a dog, etc.).

2. Brainstorm a list of reasons why you love this person, or if you chose the alternative, brainstorm possible reasons why your two objects might fall in love.

3. Read the Sample Love Poems (pages 108) and complete the Understanding Love Poems work sheet (page 109). Note the structure and effectiveness of the poems.

Drafting

Use the ideas you generated about your subject to draft a love poem. Depending on the tone of your poem, you could have a rhyming or non-rhyming poem. Use precise word choice to capture the exact message you wish to relay about your love, or the loving relationship between your two subjects.

Revising

When you have completed your draft, review your poem to make sure you have . . .

- captured the essence of the loving relationship.
- used line breaks, white space, and writing techniques to enhance the effect of your poem.
- created the tone you wish to portray.
- used precise word choices to convey your purpose.

Applying Technology

Practice using a drawing program to enhance the appearance of your text. Once you have your draft typed into the computer, draw a heart around your text using a drawing program. You could even accent the heart by using color. When you are satisfied with the appearance of your poem, print a copy.

Sample Love Poems

My Guy

My guy, he has a strong bod
Though his face is young and pure.
And though he is a little odd
for my breaking heart he's the cure.
I dream of him every night
His chocolate eyes so brown
For he is a lovely sight
From his face all the way down.
I know our worlds are far apart
But I'll always have my dreams
And I couldn't betray my lovesick heart
No matter how hopeless it seems.
I'll love my guy my whole life through
And when you find your guy,
you will too!

Commentary

How does the rhyme affect the tone of the poem?

Why does the author think their love is hopeless?

What is the author's tone?

Lovesick and Green

Once upon a time
on a green grass road
lived a snail, a slug, and a
great big toad.
The great big toad
liked the little bitty snail
but the snail liked the slug
who lived in a pail.
The slug didn't know
what the heck was going on
'til he saw the little bitty snail
watch him on the lawn.
He fell in love
in less than one hour
He married the snail
which made the toad sour.

What is the author's tone?

Understanding Love Poems

"My Guy"

1. Who is the speaker of this poem? _____

   _____

2. How do you know this? _____

3. Why do you think the author chose this particular title for the poem?_____

   _____

4. What strikes you as particularly interesting about this poem?_____

   _____

5. Which words paint the most vivid picture in your mind or create the strongest feelings?

   _____

6. What writing techniques did the author employ? _____

   _____

7. What was the author's purpose in choosing these techniques? _____

   _____

8. What is the author's tone in this poem?_____

9. Is the love poem effective?_____

10. What would you have done differently if you had written this poem? _____

    _____

"Lovesick and Green"

1. What love relationship is the author describing? _____

2. Why do you think the author chose this particular title for the poem?_____

   _____

3. What strikes you as particularly interesting about this poem?_____

   _____

4. Which words paint the most vivid picture in your mind or create the strongest feelings?

   _____

5. What writing techniques did the author employ? _____

   _____

6. What was the author's purpose in choosing these techniques? _____

   _____

7. What is the author's tone in this poem?_____

8. Is this love poem effective? _____

9. What would you have done differently if you had written this poem? _____

   _____

Idea Bank

1. Write a poem about a loving relationship between two people whom you admire.
2. Write a poem about a loving relationship in a fairy tale or other fiction story.

   _____

   _____

   _____

Memory Poems
Teacher's Guide

Definition: A *memory poem* is written about a memory the author has. It could be a happy or sad memory, a recent or old memory. As always, it is important to select appropriate words and techniques to reflect the mood of the subject.

Materials Needed: Student Assignment Sheet (page 111), Samples of Memory Poems (page 112–113), Understanding Memory Poems (page 114–115)

Preparation: Reproduce one copy of each work sheet for each student.

Lesson Plan: Review the Student Assignment Sheet with students. Tell them about the rubric that you will be using to assess their poems (shown below). Give students a deadline for turning in their assignment.

Poetry Assessment Rubric

Criteria for **excellent** memory poems:

_____ The poem clearly expresses the poet's memory and its importance.

_____ The poem evokes a strong feeling or mood.

_____ The author has strategically used white space and line breaks to create an intended effect.

_____ The author uses precise word choices to enhance the effect of the poem.

_____ The rhythm of the poem enhances the mood of the poem.

_____ The author uses writing techniques to enhance the effect of the poem.

_____ Spelling and punctuation are correct.

Criteria for **satisfactory** memory poems:

_____ The poem expresses the poet's memory and its importance.

_____ The poem evokes a strong feeling or mood.

_____ The author has considered white space and line breaks in drafting the poem.

_____ The author uses effective word choices to enhance the effect of the poem.

_____ The poem has an appropriate rhythm to match the mood of the poem.

_____ The author uses writing techniques to enhance the effect of the poem.

_____ Spelling and punctuation do not interfere with the meaning of the poem.

Criteria for **unsatisfactory** memory poems:

_____ The poem does not express the poet's memory.

_____ The poem does not evoke a feeling or mood.

_____ The author has not considered white space and line breaks in drafting the poem.

_____ The author does not use effective word choices to enhance the effect of the poem.

_____ The rhythm is inappropriate for the mood of the poem.

_____ The author does not use writing techniques to enhance the effect of the poem.

_____ Spelling and punctuation may interfere with the meaning of the poem.

Memory Poems
Student Assignment Sheet

A *memory poem* is written about a memory the author has. It could be a happy or sad memory, a recent or old memory. As always, it is important to select appropriate words and techniques to reflect the mood of the subject.

Getting Ready to Write

1. Think for a moment about some of your fondest memories. They could be memories from earlier in your childhood, of special holiday celebrations, or special people in your life. Jot down your ideas.

2. Think for a moment of more recent memories. They could be about what you did last weekend, the last game you played, or the last conversation you had with a friend. Jot down your ideas.

3. Select one of the memories that is most important to you. Brainstorm a list of things you remember about the person or event involved in your memory. List as many details as you can.

4. Read the Sample Memory Poems (pages 112–113) and complete the Understanding Memory Poems work sheets (pages 114–115). Note the structure and effectiveness of the poems.

Drafting

The best way to draft a memory poem is simply to record your thoughts and feelings. Let all your ideas out and capture them on paper. Once you have your feelings out, then go back and reread what you have written. Use your knowledge of line breaks and white space to turn your drafting into poem form. Incorporate words and techniques that will enhance the mood of the poem.

Revising

When you have completed your draft, review your poem to make sure you have . . .

- clearly expressed your memory and its importance to you.
- used line breaks, white space, and writing techniques to enhance the effect of your poem.
- created the mood you desire.
- created an appropriate rhythm for the mood of the poem.
- used precise word choices to convey your purpose.

Applying Technology

Practice selecting different colors or fonts. After you have typed your poem in a word processing program, use the mouse to highlight the entire poem. From the font features, select a color that matches the mood of your memory poem appropriately. When you have made your selection, print a copy of your poem. Your text will print in this color.

Sample Memory Poems

Paper Airplanes

Now as the day comes to an end
I lay in bed,
Thinking of the long hours
I toiled endlessly on.
Never stopping 'til I reached my
    goal.
Paper airplanes surround the
    trash can.
Old dinner dishes on my desk.
Laying by my backpack,
The reason for all my toil:
A green folder with pockets and
    clips.
POETRY written in black ink
    across the front.
My signature scribbled in the corner.
In the pockets and clips—
    a hidden talent
My best work.
I turned it in for a grade.
My eyelids are heavy.
My thoughts are black.
My head hits the pillow.
I see darkness.

Forever

There he was
alive, strong, and looking well.
I saw the happiness in his eyes
in his laughter
in his smile.
It looked like it would never fade.
As I stepped out of his door
and said goodbye
I didn't mean forever.

Commentary

This poem doesn't rhyme. How does that affect the tone of the poem?

Why did the author choose to use repetition here?

What happened? What is the author's tone?

Sample Memory Poems *(cont.)*

My Whole World

As we would walk,
she would tell me stories
of the olden days
              or
we would go see
sweet old Aunt Emma
but all the while
she was deteriorating, dying.
    She was my best friend
    my confidante
    for the first few years
        of my life.
But, how's an eight-year-old to
understand
death?
All I wanted was my grandmom
but for the first time in my
life,
I was all
alone.

Missing

Searching for a lost friend
in a place called Memory Lane
Forever, constantly searching
for us,
Our fallen tears like rain.

And when we think we've finally fixed
the problems we once had,
they start again,
we argue more—
this time it's twice as bad.

I wish I could go back in time
and tell her what she means
that she was my very best
    friend,
I remember in my dreams.

Commentary

What was the tone of this poem?

What's missing?

What is the author's tone?

What is the author trying to express?

Understanding Memory Poems

"Paper Airplanes"

1. What is the author remembering? _____

2. Why do you think the author chose this particular title for the poem?_____
   _____

3. What strikes you as particularly interesting about this poem?_____
   _____

4. Which words paint the most vivid pictures in your mind or create the strongest feelings?
   _____

5. What writing techniques did the author employ? _____
   _____

6. What was the author's purpose in choosing these techniques? _____
   _____

7. What is the author's tone in this poem?_____
   _____

8. Is this memory poem effective? _____

9. What would you have done differently if you had written this poem? _____
   _____

"Forever"

1. What is the author remembering? _____

2. Why do you think the author chose this particular title for the poem?_____
   _____

3. What strikes you as particularly interesting about this poem?_____
   _____

4. Which words paint the most vivid pictures in your mind or create the strongest feelings?
   _____

5. What writing techniques did the author employ? _____
   _____

6. What was the author's purpose in choosing these techniques? _____
   _____

7. What is the author's tone in this poem?_____

8. Is this memory poem effective? _____

9. What would you have done differently if you had written this poem? _____
   _____

Understanding Memory Poems *(cont.)*

"My Whole World"

1. What is the author remembering? _____

2. Why do you think the author chose this particular title for the poem?_____
   _____

3. What strikes you as particularly interesting about this poem?_____
   _____

4. Which words paint the most vivid pictures in your mind or create the strongest feelings?
   _____

5. What writing techniques did the author employ? _____
   _____

6. What was the author's purpose in choosing these techniques? _____
   _____

7. What is the author's tone in this poem?_____

8. Is this memory poem effective? _____

9. What would you have done differently if you had written this poem? _____
   _____

"Missing"

1. What is the author remembering? _____

2. Why do you think the author chose this particular title for the poem?_____
   _____

3. What strikes you as particularly interesting about this poem?_____
   _____

4. Which words paint the most vivid pictures in your mind or create the strongest feelings?
   _____

5. What writing techniques did the author employ? _____
   _____

6. What was the author's purpose in choosing these techniques? _____
   _____

7. What is the author's tone in this poem?_____

8. Is this memory poem effective? _____

9. What would you have done differently if you had written this poem? _____
   _____

Idea Bank

1. Look through magazines or newspaper articles for the reminiscences of a well-known person whom you admire. Use their name as a title, then write a poem using that person's memory as content.

2. Ask someone much younger than you for a memory. Use that child's memory as the basis for a poem.

   _____

   _____

Photo Poems
Teacher's Guide

Definition: A *photo poem* uses a photograph as a prompt for writing. The photo should portray a person, particular capturing the person's face. The author of a photo poem uses precise word choice to capture the person's appearance in words, just as the photographer captured the person on film.

Materials Needed: Student Assignment Sheet (page 117), Generating Words from Pictures (page 118), Samples of Photo Poems (page 119), Understanding Photo Poems (page 120)

Preparation: Reproduce one copy of each work sheet for each student.

Lesson Plan: Review the Student Assignment Sheet with students. Tell them about the rubric that you will be using to assess their poetry (shown below). Give students a deadline for turning in their assignment.

Poetry Assessment Rubric

Criteria for **excellent** photo poems:

_____ The poem clearly captures the appearance of the subject.

_____ The author has strategically used white space and line breaks to create an intended effect.

_____ The author uses precise word choices to enhance the effect of the poem.

_____ The author uses writing techniques to enhance the effect of the poem.

_____ Spelling and punctuation are correct.

Criteria for **satisfactory** photo poems:

_____ The poem captures the appearance of the subject.

_____ The author has considered white space and line breaks in drafting the poem.

_____ The author uses effective word choices to enhance the effect of the poem.

_____ The author uses some writing techniques that enhance the effect of the poem.

_____ Spelling and punctuation do not interfere with the meaning of the poem.

Criteria for **unsatisfactory** photo poems:

_____ The poem does not capture the appearance of the subject.

_____ The author has not considered white space and line breaks in drafting the poem.

_____ The author does not use effective word choice to enhance the effect of the poem.

_____ The author does not use writing techniques to enhance the effect of the poem.

_____ Spelling and punctuation may interfere with the meaning of the poem.

Photo Poems
Student Assignment Sheet

A *photo poem* uses a photograph as a prompt for writing. The photo should portray a person, particularly capturing the person's face. The author of a photo poem uses precise word choice to capture the person's appearance in words, just as the photographer captured the person on film.

Getting Ready to Write

1. Select a picture of a person you know or a face that interests you.

2. Using the Generating Words from Pictures work sheet (page 118), brainstorm a description of the person's face.

3. Read the Sample Photo Poems (page 119) and complete the Understanding Photo Poems work sheet (page 120). Note the structure and effectiveness of the poems.

Drafting

Use the ideas you generated about your subject to draft your photo poem. Depending on the tone of your poem, you could have a rhyming or non-rhyming poem. Use precise word choice to capture the exact appearance of your subject.

Revising

When you have completed your draft, review your poem to make sure you have . . .

- captured the appearance of your subject.

- used line breaks, white space, and writing techniques to enhance the effect of your poem.

- created the tone you wish to portray.

- used precise word choices to convey your purpose.

Applying Technology:

Practice using a scanner. Once you have your draft typed into the computer, scan the photo of your subject and insert it into your document. When you are satisfied with the appearance of your poem and the scanned photo, print a copy.

Generating Words from Pictures

Directions: Study the photograph or picture of the person you have chosen as the basis for your photo poem. Use this work sheet to generate ideas about the person's appearance. Try to be as descriptive as you can.

Describe the person's hair.

_____
_____
_____
_____
_____
_____
_____

Describe the person's eyes.

_____
_____
_____
_____
_____
_____
_____

Describe the person's nose.

_____
_____
_____
_____
_____
_____
_____

Describe the person's mouth.

_____
_____
_____
_____
_____
_____
_____

Describe the person's skin.

_____
_____
_____
_____
_____
_____
_____

Describe the person's overall face.

_____
_____
_____
_____
_____
_____
_____

Sample Photo Poems

Marc Antony

How strong that face,
How dark that hair,
    his eyes, they bore right
    through and stare.
Coal-black, they are
    they see through me
His skin, to the touch
    is oh, so sweet.
His nose, quite little, like a
    button
His lips are pink, and juicy as
    fruit
His smile curves up, he breaks a
    grin.
Glistening teeth attend and
    salute.

Ariel

Her hair is like ocean waves
cascading on the shore.
Her eyes are glistening
seashells, waiting to be
explored.
Her nose stands straight and
tall, a proud lighthouse in the
mist.
Her mouth envelopes the natural
world, and holds it in its kiss.

Commentary

Where did this title come from?

Note the rhyme scheme.

Here is a simile.

What does this last line mean?

Where did this title come from?
Here is a simile with elaboration.
Here is a metaphor with elaboration.

Here is another metaphor.

What is the author's tone?

Understanding Photo Poems

"Marc Antony"

1. Whom is the author describing? _____
2. Why do you think the author chose this particular title for the poem?_____
   _____
3. What strikes you as particularly interesting about this poem?_____
   _____
4. Which words paint the most vivid pictures in your mind or create the strongest feelings?
   _____
5. What writing techniques did the author employ? _____
   _____
6. What was the author's purpose in choosing these techniques? _____
   _____
7. Is the photo poem effective? _____
8. What would you have done differently if you had written this poem? _____
   _____

"Ariel"

1. Whom is the author describing? _____
2. Why do you think the author chose this particular title for the poem?_____
   _____
3. What strikes you as particularly interesting about this poem?_____
   _____
4. Which words paint the most vivid pictures in your mind or create the strongest feelings?
   _____
5. What writing techniques did the author employ? _____
   _____
6. What was the author's purpose in choosing these techniques? _____
   _____
7. Is this photo poem effective? _____
8. What would you have done differently if you had written this poem? _____
   _____

Idea Bank

1. Have a photo session with your friends or relatives. Write a poem about the experience of taking photographs.
2. Look through a book of historical information for a reproduction of an old photograph. Write a poem about the face in the photo.
3. Use the lines below to capture your own ideas for photo poems.

   _____
   _____
   _____
   _____

Preposition Poems
Teacher's Guide

Definition: A *preposition poem* is one in which each line begins with a preposition. The lines are written as phrases and provide a sequence of steps or events.

Materials Needed: Student Assignment Sheet (page 122); Prepositions (page 123); Sample Preposition Poems (page 124); Understanding Preposition Poems (page 125)

Preparation: Reproduce one copy of each work sheet for each student.

Lesson Plan: Review the Student Assignment Sheet with students. Tell students about the rubric that you will be using to assess their poetry (shown below). Give students a deadline for turning in their assignments.

Poetry Assessment Rubric

Criteria for **excellent** preposition poems:

_____ The poem clearly focuses on a topic.

_____ The author has begun each line with a preposition.

_____ The author uses precise word choices to enhance the effect of the poem.

_____ Spelling and punctuation are correct.

Criteria for **satisfactory** preposition poems:

_____ The poem focuses on a topic.

_____ The author has begun each line with a preposition.

_____ The author uses effective word choices to enhance the effect of the poem.

_____ Spelling and punctuation do not interfere with the meaning of the poem.

Criteria for **unsatisfactory** preposition poems:

_____ The poem does not focus on the topic.

_____ The author does not begin each line with a preposition.

_____ The author does not use effective word choices that does not enhance the effect of the poem.

_____ Spelling and punctuation may interfere with the meaning of the poem.

Writing a Preposition Poem
Student Assignment Sheet

A *preposition poem* is one in which each line begins with a preposition. The lines are written as phrases and provide a sequence of steps or events.

Getting Ready to Write

1. Choose a topic by thinking of a familiar location. Jot down directions from a starting point of your choice to your familiar location. For example, you could give directions from your front door to your bedroom, from the grocery store to the post office, from your math classroom to the cafeteria, etc.

   Alternatively, think of an action (e.g., pitching a baseball), an event (e.g., a parade), or a chore (e.g., making a peanut butter and jelly sandwich). List the sequence of steps that occur as components of the action or event. For example, if you chose pitching a baseball, you might write the following:

   > *Pick up the ball*
   > *Put it in glove*
   > *Toss chalk bag*
   > *Throw it to the ground*
   > *Hold the baseball in the glove*
   > *Concentrate . . .*

2. Read the Sample Preposition Poems (page 124) and complete the Understanding Preposition Poems worksheet (page 125). Note the structure and effectiveness of the poems.

Drafting

Revise your jotted lists by beginning each step with a preposition. You may need to use the Prepositions worksheet (page 123) for assistance generating prepositions. You also may have to rearrange your wording within each step so that it makes sense.

Revising

When you have completed your draft, review your poem to make sure you have . . .

- begun each line with a preposition.
- used line breaks, white space, and writing techniques to enhance the effect of your poem.
- used precise word choices to convey your purpose.

Applying Technology

Practice using the underline, bold, or italics function. Use your mouse to highlight the first word of each line (the preposition). Select either underline, bold, or italics to change the style of the font on the first word. When you are satisfied with the effect, print a copy of your poem.

Prepositions

Definition: A *preposition* is a word used to show the relationship between words. Here is a list of commonly used prepositions.

- about
- above
- across
- after
- against
- along
- amid
- among
- around
- at
- before
- behind
- below
- beneath
- beside
- besides
- between
- beyond
- by
- concerning
- down
- during
- except

- for
- from
- in
- into
- like
- of
- on
- over
- past
- since
- through
- throughout
- to
- toward
- under
- underneath
- until
- unto
- up
- upon
- with
- within
- without

Sample Preposition Poems

Moon Gazing

Above the ground
In the sky
Over everyone and everything
Out of the darkness
Through the clouds
Onto my face the moon reflects.

Shopping

Out of the car
In my arms
Through the doorway
On the carpet
In the kitchen
Among the appliances
Out of the bag
In the refrigerator
Out of the bag
In the cupboard
Out of the bag
Into the pantry

Fourth of July

In a straight line
Down the street
Through the town
Around the corner
Past the houses
Beside the people
Near the edge
Toward the end
From the parade, the sound fades
    away.

Commentary

What is the author's purpose?

What is happening in this poem?
What is the author's purpose?

What is happening in this poem?

Understanding Preposition Poems

"Moon Gazing"

1. What is the author writing about? _____

2. Why do you think the author chose this particular title for the poem?_____
_____

3. What strikes you as particularly interesting about this poem?_____
_____

4. Is this preposition poem effective? _____

5. What would you have done differently if you had written this poem? _____
_____

"Shopping"

1. What is the author writing about? _____

2. Why do you think the author chose this particular title for the poem?_____
_____

3. What strikes you as particularly interesting about this poem?_____
_____

4. Is this preposition poem effective? _____
_____

5. What would you have done differently if you had written this poem? _____
_____

"Fourth of July"

1. What is the author writing about? _____

2. Why do you think the author chose this particular title for the poem?_____
_____

3. What strikes you as particularly interesting about this poem?_____
_____

4. Is this preposition poem effective? _____
_____

5. What would you have done differently if you had written this poem? _____
_____

Idea Bank

1. Look over your collection of poems. Are there any poems that might be more interesting if they were written with lines that begin with prepositions?

2. Use the lines below to capture any ideas for preposition poems.

_____

_____

_____

_____

Self-Expression Poems
Teacher's Guide

Definition: A *self-expression poem* is about yourself. It could be a physical description of yourself. It could be a poem about your inner thoughts, fears, dreams, etc. It could be a look into your personality or hobbies. You can write a self-expression poem any way you want—it's about you!

Materials Needed: Student Assignment Sheet (page 127), Samples of Self-Expression Poems (pages 128–129), Understanding Self-Expression Poems (page 130–131)

Preparation: Reproduce one copy of each work sheet for each student.

Lesson Plan: Review the Student Assignment Sheet with students. Tell students the rubric that you will be using to assess their poetry (shown below). Give students a deadline for turning in their assignment.

Poetry Assessment

Criteria for **excellent** self-expression poems:

_____ The poem clearly expresses the poet's voice or character.
_____ The poem evokes a strong feeling or mood.
_____ The author has strategically used white space and line breaks to create an intended effect.
_____ The author uses precise word choices to enhance the effect of the poem.
_____ The author uses writing techniques to enhance the effect of the poem.
_____ Spelling and punctuation are correct.

Criteria for **satisfactory** self-expression poems:

_____ The poem expresses the poet's voice or character.
_____ The poem evokes a feeling or mood.
_____ The author has considered white space and line breaks in drafting the poem.
_____ The author uses effective word choices to enhance the effect of the poem.
_____ The author uses writing techniques to enhance the effect of the poem.
_____ Spelling and punctuation do not interfere with the meaning of the poem.

Criteria for **unsatisfactory** self-expression poems:

_____ The poem does not express the poet's voice or character.
_____ The poem does not evoke a feeling or mood.
_____ The author has not considered white space and line breaks in drafting the poem.
_____ The author does not use effective word choices to enhance the effect of the poem.
_____ The author does not use writing techniques to enhance the effect of the poem.
_____ Spelling and punctuation may interfere with the meaning of the poem.

Self-Expression Poems
Student Assignment Sheet

A *self-expression poem* is about yourself. It could be a physical description of yourself. It could be a poem about your inner thoughts, fears, dreams, etc. It could be a look into your personality or hobbies. You can write a self-expression poem any way you want to—it's about you!

Getting Ready to Write

1. Think about your hobbies. Think about your looks. Think about your interests. Think about your hopes, your dreams, and your curiosities. Think about your pet peeves and your insecurities. Think about your fears. Think about who you are.

2. Read Sample Self-Expression Poems (pages 128–129) and complete the Understanding Self-Expression Poems work sheets (pages 130–131). Note the structure and effectiveness of the poems.

3. Write. Once you have an idea for a topic, just write. Don't worry about poem form. Don't worry about it sounding good. Don't think—just write.

Drafting

Reread what you wrote. Using your knowledge of line breaks and white space, create a poem out of your brainstormed writing. Incorporate poetic language—precise word choices, writing techniques—to enhance your poem.

Revising

When you have completed your draft, review your poem to make sure you have . . .

- clearly captured your spirit and expressed what you wanted to express.

- used line breaks, white space, and writing techniques to enhance the effect of your poem.

- created the tone you desire.

- used precise choices to convey your purpose.

Applying Technology

Use a drawing or painting program to illustrate your poem. Since this is a self-expression poem, illustrate it any way you like. Remember, you are expressing yourself. Be creative! When you are happy with the finished product, print a copy of your poem and artwork.

Sample Self-Expression Poems

Does Tall = Basketball?

Just because I am tall
Do I have to play basketball?
Everyone says that I should play
That I could be a star one day
That I could get a scholarship
But I just have to say,
    "Thanks for the tip."
You see, I don't want to play basketball
'cause I might end up in a mall
signing autographs when
my career is dead.
Sorry. I'd rather have an
education instead.

Commentary

The rhythm of this poem is a little off. How could it be fixed?

What is the author's tone?

The Blue Ribbon

Life is a contest that I am in,
I try my hardest but cannot win.
He'd make it higher if I
    reached his goal,
It isn't fair, not logical.
"Stand tall, upright, look your
    best,
You have to be better than all
the rest!"
Will I ever meet his
    expectations?
Honestly, what's the use?
I try my hardest, why can't he see?
I am not perfect?
Neither is he.

Who is the speaker?

Who is the "he?"

What is the author's tone?

Sample Self-Expression Poems *(cont.)*

The Magical Stream

I go to the magical stream,
And it is so peaceful there.
Seems just like a dream
I have not a worry or care.

I get there and feel warm inside
And I talk about anything
At the stream I have nothing
    to hide.

Sometimes that includes crying.

The water reflects the sunlight
And then I start to feel good
It is a very magical sight
The stream cheers me up better
 than anyone could.

The water ripples with the wind
And the trees seem to say "hi"
I think I never want this
feeling to end
As the birds chirp and fly by.

It is really a special spot
And it is a great place to go.
I know its beauty, some do not.
But this is where I go when I'm
feeling low.

This is my magical stream.

Commentary

Note the ABAB rhyme scheme.

Why is this line by itself?

The rhythm is a little off in this line. How could it be fixed?

Understanding Self-Expression Poems

"Does Tall = Basketball?"

1. What is the author expressing? _____

   _____

2. What kind of person do you think the author is? _____

   _____

3. Why do you think the author chose this particular title for the poem? _____

   _____

4. What strikes you as particularly interesting about this poem? _____

   _____

5. Which words paint the most vivid picture in your mind? _____

   _____

6. What writing techniques did the author employ? _____

   _____

7. What was the author's purpose in choosing these techniques? _____

   _____

8. Is this self-expression poem effective? _____

9. What would you have done differently if you had written this poem? _____

   _____

"The Blue Ribbon"

1. What is the author expressing? _____

   _____

2. What kind of person do you think the author is? _____

   _____

3. Why do you think the author chose this particular title for the poem? _____

   _____

4. What strikes you as particularly interesting about this poem? _____

   _____

5. Which words paint the most vivid picture in your mind? _____

   _____

6. What writing techniques did the author employ? _____

   _____

7. What was the author's purpose in choosing these techniques? _____

   _____

8. Is this self-expression poem effective? _____

9. What would you have done differently if you had written this poem? _____

   _____

Understanding Self-Expression Poems *(cont.)*

"The Magical Stream"

1. What is the author expressing? _____

   _____

2. What kind of person do you think the author is? _____

   _____

3. Why do you think the author chose this particular title for the poem? _____

   _____

4. What strikes you as particularly interesting about this poem? _____

   _____

5. Which words paint the most vivid picture in your mind? _____

   _____

6. What writing techniques did the author employ? _____

   _____

7. What was the author's purpose in choosing these techniques? _____

   _____

8. Is this self-expression poem effective? _____

   _____

9. What would you have done differently if you had written this poem? _____

   _____

Idea Bank

1. Look through your journal, if you keep one, for ideas for poems about your pet peeves.

2. Write a poem about some tiny aspect about yourself that no one else really knows, such as needing to have the seam in your socks just so or letting your cereal get soggy with milk before you like to eat it.

3. Use the lines below to capture your own ideas for self-expression poems.

   _____

   _____

   _____

   _____

   _____

   _____

   _____

Sensory Poems
Teacher's Guide

Definition: A *sensory poem* uses vivid words to create a sensory impression in the reader's mind. Sensory poems are most interesting when they stimulate more than one sense; that is, the reader can see, hear, taste, smell, and feel the subject being described in the poem.

Materials Needed: Student Assignment Sheet (page 133), Samples of Sensory Poems (page 134), Understanding Sensory Poems (page 135)

Preparation: Reproduce one copy of each work sheet for each student.

Lesson Plan: Review the Student Assignment Sheet with students. Tell them about the rubric that you will be using to assess their poetry, shown below. Give students a deadline for turning in their assignment.

Poetry Assessment Rubric

Criteria for **excellent** sensory poems:

_____ The poem clearly focuses on the topic.

_____ The author uses strong sensory words to create a vivid impression.

_____ The author has strategically used white space and line breaks to create an intended effect.

_____ The author uses precise word choices to enhance the effect of the poem.

_____ The author uses writing techniques to enhance the effect of the poem.

_____ Spelling and punctuation are correct.

Criteria for **satisfactory** sensory poems:

_____ The poem focuses on the topic.

_____ The author uses sensory words to create an impression.

_____ The author has considered white space and line breaks in drafting the poem.

_____ The author uses effective word choices to enhance the effect of the poem.

_____ The author uses writing techniques to enhance the effect of the poem.

_____ Spelling and punctuation do not interfere with the meaning of the poem.

Criteria for **unsatisfactory** sensory poems:

_____ The poem does not focus on the topic.

_____ The author does not uses sensory words to create an impression.

_____ The author has not considered white space and line breaks in drafting the poem.

_____ The author does not use effective word choices to enhance the effect of the poem.

_____ The author does not use writing techniques to enhance the effect of the poem.

_____ Spelling and punctuation may interfere with the meaning of the poem.

Sensory Poems
Student Assignment Sheet

A *sensory poem* uses vivid words to create a sensory impression in the reader's mind. Sensory poems are most interesting when they stimulate more than one sense; that is, the reader can see, hear, taste, smell, and feel the subject being described in the poem.

Getting Ready to Write

1. Close your eyes and imagine that you are eating your favorite food. Pick it up. Look at it. What does it look like? How does your mouth react to the sight of this food? Smell the food. What scents do you recognize? How does your mouth react to smelling it? Open your mouth and take a bite. How does it feel in your mouth? What tastes do you recognize? How does it make you feel? Swallow the food. How does it feel in your stomach?

2. Now, open your eyes and jot down your ideas as quickly as you can. Try to recall all of the sensory details.

3. Read the Sample Sensory Poems (page 134) and complete the Understanding Sensory Poems work sheet (page 135). Note the structure and effectiveness of the poems.

Drafting

Use your list of details to draft a sensory poem. If you'd prefer to use a different topic, you may. Just make sure that you have sufficient detail to create a sensory poem. Try to use the most precise word choice you can. Try to appeal to all of the senses—sight, sound, smell, taste, and touch.

Revising

When you have completed your draft, review your poem to make sure you have . . .

- focused on your topic.
- used line breaks, white space, and writing techniques to enhance the effect of your poem.
- created the tone you wish to portray.
- used precise word choices to convey your purpose.

Applying Technology

Practice using the thesaurus feature on your computer. As you draft your poem and encounter a boring word, select the thesaurus feature to view several options for replacing it. Be sure you understand the subtle shades of meaning among words to make sure you choose the right word.

Sample Sensory Poems

Ashes

Waves of flickering sparks
Lap over the weathered lumber.
Crackling and burning
The red hot sheets of fire
Dance toward the sky.
Frenzied flashes
Of vibrant colors
Wash over the
Charred logs.
In time
This will all be
A smoldering pile of ashes.

Commentary

This shows great word choice—
very vivid and specific.
Here is the use of onomatopoeia.
"Sheets of fire" is a good metaphor.
Here is the use of personification.
Here is the use of alliteration.

The poem shows a progression through time.
The words in the beginning are strong and
energetic; toward the end they become more
mellow.

Sweetness

Speared through its side
the gummy sweetness is thrust
into flames
The bright orange
and yellow heat
licks hungrily at it.
Puffing out,
it rises a little
almost out of the flames
the lightness of it turns tan,
then chestnut,
then charcoal black.
its crispy sides are brushed
away to reveal the gooey
marshmallow inside.

This sounds like a battle, but the next line makes
the reader wonder what the subject is.

Here is the use of personification.

Specific colors are used here.

Here are texture words: gummy, crispy, gooey.

Understanding Sensory Poems

"Ashes"

1. What is the author describing? _____
2. Why do you think the author chose this particular title for the poem?_____
   _____
3. What strikes you as particularly interesting about this poem?_____
   _____
4. Which words paint the most vivid picture in your mind? _____
   _____
5. What writing techniques did the author employ? _____
6. What was the author's purpose in choosing these techniques? _____
   _____
7. Is this sensory poem effective? _____
8. What would you have done differently if you had written this poem? _____
   _____

"Sweetness"

1. What is the author describing? _____
2. Why do you think the author chose this particular title for the poem?_____
   _____
3. What strikes you as particularly interesting about this poem?_____
   _____
4. Which words paint the most vivid picture in your mind? _____
   _____
5. What writing techniques did the author employ? _____
6. What was the author's purpose in choosing these techniques? _____
   _____
7. Is this sensory poem effective? _____
8. What would you have done differently if you had written this poem? _____
   _____

Idea Bank

1. Think of a place with evocative smells, such as the food court in a mall or a fabulous garden. Write a poem describing the various scents.
2. Listen to a piece of music that you enjoy. Write a poem describing the feelings that the music evokes in you.
3. Use the lines below to capture your ideas about sensory poems.

_____
_____
_____
_____
_____
_____

Snapshot Poems
Teacher's Guide

Definition: A *snapshot poem* describes a picture or a particular scene. Its purpose is to enable the reader to visualize the scene without actually seeing it.

Materials Needed: Student Assignment Sheet (page 137), Sample Snapshot Poems (pages 138–139), Understanding Snapshot Poems (page 140)

Preparation: Reproduce one copy of each work sheet for each student.

Lesson Plan: Review the Student Assignment Sheet with students. Tell students about the rubric that you will be using to assess their poetry (shown below). Give students a deadline for turning in their assignment.

Poetry Assessment

Criteria for **excellent** snapshot poems:

_____   The poem clearly focuses on the scene portrayed in the picture prompt.

_____   The poem evokes strong sensory images.

_____   The poem evokes a strong feeling or mood.

_____   The author has strategically used white space and line breaks to create an intended effect.

_____   The author uses precise word choices to enhance the effect of the poem.

_____   The author uses writing techniques to enhance the effect of the poem.

_____   Spelling and punctuation are correct.

Criteria for **satisfactory** snapshot poems:

_____   The poem focuses on the scene portrayed in the picture prompt.

_____   The poem evokes sensory images.

_____   The poem evokes a feeling or mood.

_____   The author has considered white space and line breaks in drafting the poem.

_____   The author uses effective word choices to enhance the effect of the poem.

_____   The author uses writing techniques to enhance the effect of the poem.

_____   Spelling and punctuation do not interfere with the meaning of the poem.

Criteria for **unsatisfactory** snapshot poems:

_____   The poem does not focus on the scene portrayed in the picture prompt.

_____   The poem does not evoke sensory images.

_____   The poem does not evoke a feeling or mood.

_____   The author has not considered white space and line breaks in drafting the poem.

_____   The author does not use effective word choices to enhance the effect of the poem.

_____   The author does not use writing techniques to enhance the effect of the poem.

Writing a Snapshot Poem
Student Assignment Sheet

> A *snapshot poem* describes a picture or a particular scene. Its purpose is to enable the reader to visualize the scene without actually seeing it.

Getting Ready to Write

1. Select a picture that interests you. It could be from a newspaper, magazine, or personal photograph. You could even use a live scene that you have witnessed.

2. Write a paragraph that vividly describes the picture. Be sure to use the most specific, effective words possible. You want the reader to be able to visualize the scene without actually seeing it.

3. Read the Sample Snapshot Poems (pages 138–139) and complete Understanding Snapshot Poems (page 140). Note the structure and effectiveness of the poems.

Drafting

Read your paragraph aloud. Listen for natural breaks and pauses. Determine your most powerful words. You will want to emphasize them in your snapshot poem. Using your knowledge of line breaks and white space, turn your descriptive paragraph into a poem.

Revising

When you have completed your draft, review your poem to make sure you have . . .

- vividly captured the scene with words.

- used precise word choices to convey your purpose.

Applying Technology

Practice scanning a picture to accompany your text. Using the picture you selected as your writing prompt, scan it into your word processing document. You can change the size of the picture after it is scanned into the computer. Once you are satisfied with the effect of the photo and your text, print a copy.

Sample Snapshot Poems

Original Paragraph

The gently sloping grass frames the mountainside majestically. The sun burns down on the mountaintop snow, making it shine like a pile of diamonds. Down below is a valley littered with colorful flowers and small trees. To the right is a brightly lit town, alive with people and music. To the left is a secluded forest, lying silent as a tomb.

Poem

Serenity

The gently sloping grass
frames the mountainside
    majestically.
The sun burns down
on the mountaintop snow,
making it shine like a pile of
    diamonds.
Down below is a valley
littered with colorful flowers
and
small
trees.
    To the right
    is a brightly lit town,
    alive with people
    and music.
To the left
is a secluded forest,
lying silent as a
tomb.

Commentary

Notice the descriptive language.

Notice the simile used here.

Does the word "littered" fit in with the overall tone of the poem? Can you think of a better word?

Why is this stanza moved over to the right and the following one kept to the left?

Sample Snapshot Poems *(cont.)*

Original Paragraph

Lonesome trees sit in the pale morning light, guarding the shores of a peaceful pond. A hazy mist hangs over the trees and the dew-covered grass like a veil. Faintly, in the distance, the howl of a dog and the mellow trickling of a stream echoes through the empty valley. I sit in the midst of the saddened trees wondering why they mourn.

Poem

Sitting in Sorrow

Lonesome
    trees
sit in the pale morning
light,
guarding the shores
of a peaceful pond.
  A hazy mist
  hangs
over the trees and the
dew-covered grass
like a veil.
F a i n t l y,
     in the distance
the howl of a dog
and the mellow trickling
of a stream
echoes

through the empty valley.
I sit in the midst of
the saddened trees
wondering why
they mourn.

Commentary

This is interesting personification, as trees aren't often thought of as "lonely."

Here is another use of personification.

Here is the use of simile.

Why did the poet space the word faintly like this?

Why did the poet leave a blank line after echoes?

Notice the interesting word play with mist *above and the word* midst *used here.*

This is a thoughtful, interesting ending with personification: Who would think of trees mourning?

Understanding Snapshot Poems

"Serenity"

1. What is the author describing? _____
2. Why do you think the author chose this particular title for the poem?_____
_____
3. What strikes you as particularly interesting about this poem?_____
_____
4. Which words paint the most vivid pictures in your mind? _____
_____
5. What writing techniques did the author employ? _____
_____
6. What was the author's purpose in choosing these techniques? _____
_____
7. Is this snapshot poem effective? _____
8. What would you have done differently if you had written this poem? _____
_____

"Sitting in Sorrow"

1. What is the author describing? _____
2. Why do you think the author chose this particular title for the poem?_____
_____
3. What strikes you as particularly interesting about this poem?_____
_____
4. Which words paint the most vivid pictures in your mind? _____
_____
5. What writing techniques did the author employ? _____
_____
6. What was the author's purpose in choosing these techniques? _____
_____
7. Is this snapshot poem effective? _____
8. What would you have done differently if you had written this poem? _____
_____

Idea Bank

1. Visit an actual place and write a description of it. Turn your description into a snapshot poem so that readers can visualize the place.
2. Write a paragraph about a place in your imagination. Turn your paragraph into a snapshot poem.
3. Use the lines below to capture your own ideas about snapshot poems.

_____
_____
_____
_____

Compiling a Poetry Portfolio
Student Assignment Sheet

Now that you have written many poems, it is time to showcase your best work. You will need to follow these steps to compile a portfolio of your best poems.

1. Review all the poems you have written.

2. Select at least 10 of your best poems to include in your portfolio.

3. Write both an introductory and a summarizing poem for your collection (see page 142 and 143). These poems will be the first and last poems in your collection. That means you will now have at least 12 poems in your portfolio.

4. Complete a cover letter for your portfolio (see page 144).

5. Include highlight notes with your poems to showcase your skills (see below).

6. Give your portfolio a title. You could use the title of one of your poems as the title of the whole portfolio or you could create a new title that captures the spirit of your writing.

7. Design a cover page for your portfolio. You could illustrate it by hand or use a graphics program on a computer. Be sure to include the title of your portfolio and your name on your cover page.

8. Put your portfolio in this order:
   - cover page
   - cover letter
   - introductory poem
   - at least 10 of your best poems with highlight notes
   - summarizing poem

9. Turn in your portfolio by _____.
   (deadline)

Writing Highlight Notes

In addition to collecting your poems, you need to write highlight notes for them. Highlight notes are notes written in the margins of text to point out items of significance to the reader. When you write highlight notes, you want to show your teacher everything that you have learned. If you used a simile in a poem (for example, "The ocean was as calm as a sleeping giant"), your note could say, "Notice the use of a simile to expand the description of the ocean." If you used an oxymoron (for example, "deafening silence"), you could point out why you used that particular technique in your poem. For your portfolio, you can write your highlight notes on sticky notes and place them in the margins of your poems. That way, your final copy will remain clean.

Sample Introductory Poems

Introductory poems are written to introduce the reader to a poetry collection. The poem could be about something beginning, something that is young or new. It could also be a poem that gives the reader a glimpse of what is to come in your poems. Here are some examples of introductory poems.

The Trail of Life

A rose's last petal wilts to the ground
As a newborn colt makes its first sound.

The sky turns violet as the crimson sun lies
And a young mother smiles as her little one cries.

A shiny penny turns from copper to green
While Daddy's little girl turns seventeen.

The end is a beginning, and the beginning is an end.
It's called the trail of life. Come with me, my friend.

A Time to Begin

Flowers bloom in the spring
An artist starts his first picture
A healthy breakfast to get the day going
The sun as it rises
January starting a fresh new year
A baby as it open its eyes for the first time
September, the month school starts
Dawn, a new day of life.

Poetic Dreams

And so begins a saga of a writer yet to be.
I will be a poet, just you wait and see.
In the stanzas to come my thoughts tell the truth
Of what I have learned about from my youth.
I write about my life as I know it,
And everything that comes naturally.
I write about how I see myself,
I even stopped to write about a tree.
So, come and take a look, my friend, of memories in my mind,
That I have gathered together through my entire lifetime.

Sample Summarizing Poems

Summarizing poems are written to conclude your poetry collection. The poem could be about something ending, something that is old or extinct, or it could be a poem that summarizes the poems in your portfolio. Here are some examples of summarizing poems.

A Time to End

Flowers wither up tight
An artist finishes his last picture
A healthy dinner to end the day
The sun as it sets
December, ending the year
June, the month school ends
Dusk, the end of the day.
A person closes his eyes for the last time.

May Your Life

May your life be like spaghetti:
Long and full of dough.
May it be topped off with love
From everyone you know.
    May your life be like ice cream:
    Sweet, rich, and creamy.
    May joy be sprinkled into your life
    And may you always be free and dreamy.
May your life be like a French fry:
Crisp and golden brown.
And even when salt gets in your wounds,
May you smile, not frown.
    May your life be like a good restaurant:
    Excellent service, although it might be late.
    And may you always think of life
    As a full plate.

Poetic Truths

And here ends the saga of a writer who has grown.
I'm a successful author, now my work is known.
In these pieces you have read, my thoughts and skills have proved to you
The many things I have learned and what I know and knew.
I wrote about my life and love.
It came so naturally!
The very many pieces are a wide variety.
So now that you have seen all that I can do,
I hope you liked my magazine,
Brought from me to you.

Portfolio Cover Letter

Date _____

Dear _____,
(Teacher's name)

Here is my portfolio entitled _____.

It includes _____ of my best poems. The poem of which I
(put number here)

am most proud is _____. I feel this

way because _____.

The hardest part of writing poetry was _____.

The easiest part was _____.

I feel that I have grown as a writer by _____.

Your student,

_____

Have a parent or relative complete the following information.

Date _____

I enjoyed reading _____'s poetry portfolio. My

favorite poem was _____.

I liked it because _____. I think he/she has

grown as a writer by _____

_____.

Sincerely,

_____